Project 2025 - A Citizen's Guide to Saving American Democracy

Uncover the Plan, Safeguard Your Rights, Secure America's Future

Emily Carter Lee

Copyright ©2024

Emily Carter Lee

All rights reserved. No part of this publication may be reproduced, stored in a retrieval system, or transmitted in any form or by any means, electronic, mechanical, photocopying, recording, or otherwise, without the written permission of the publisher. Exceptions are made for reviewers who may quote brief passages in a review published in a newspaper, magazine, or website.

Publisher: (Emily Carter Lee)

Edition: 2024

Table of Contents

INTRODUCTION — 1

CHAPTER 1 — 3
Understanding Project 2025 — 3
- Introduction to the Key Components of Project 2025 — 3
- Goals of the Initiative — 5
- Historical Context and Background — 7
- Primary Stakeholders and Their Motivations — 9
- Initial Reactions and Controversies Surrounding the Proposal — 11

CHAPTER 2 — 13
The Blueprint: Legislative and Social Changes — 13
- Key Legislative Reforms Proposed — 13
- Impact on Social Policies and Public Welfare — 15
- Future Implications for Healthcare and Education — 17
- Economic Impacts and Job Market Shifts — 19
  - Projected Economic Changes and Potential Shifts in the Job Market under Project 2025 — 19
- New Enforcement Mechanisms — 21
- Insights and Implications — 23

CHAPTER 3 — 24
Unpacking Potential Risks — 24
- Erosion of Civil Liberties — 24
- Challenges to Judicial Independence — 26
- Impacts on Free Speech and Press Freedoms — 28
- Possible International Repercussions — 29
- Socio-Political Polarization — 31

CHAPTER 4 — 34
Your Rights: Identifying Threats — 34
- Freedom of Assembly and Association — 34
  - Overview of Constitutional Guarantees Related to Assembly and Association — 34
  - Recent Legislative Actions Threatening These Rights — 35
  - Analysis of Contemporary Threats, Including Laws Limiting Protests — 35
  - Strategies for Community Mobilization and Legal Recourse — 36
- Voter Suppression Tactics — 36
- Attacks on Privacy Rights — 38
- Threats to Minority Protections — 40
- Future Outlook on Civil Liberties — 41
  - Projections on Assembly and Association Rights Future Trends — 42
  - Examination of the Evolving Landscape of Voter Suppression — 42
  - Impact of New Technologies on Monitoring and Privacy Rights — 43
  - Role of Social Movements in Shaping Future Protections — 43

CHAPTER 5 — 45
Empowerment Through Knowledge — 45

    Basic Principles of the U.S. Constitution   45
    Functioning of Federal and State Governments   47
    Role of Civic Organizations and Institutions   49
    Navigating Legal Rights and Resources Available   50
    Checks and Balances in Practice   52

CHAPTER 6   55
Practical Engagement Strategies   55
    Registering to vote and participating in elections   55
    Joining civic groups and community organizations   57
    Lobbying and direct advocacy techniques   59
    Engaging with local and national representatives   60
    Staying informed and mobilizing others   62

CHAPTER 7   65
Organizing Your Community   65
    Building a Grassroots Movement   65
    Effective Communication and Messaging   68
    Hosting Events and Rallies   70
    Forming Coalitions and Alliances   72
    Utilizing Local Resources   73

CHAPTER 8   76
Navigating Misinformation   76
    Recognizing misinformation and disinformation   76
    Critical media literacy skills   78
    Reliable sources for accurate information   80
    Combatting fake news and propaganda   82
    The impact of misinformation on democracy   84

CHAPTER 9   87
Using Digital Tools for Advocacy   87
    Social Media as a Tool for Activism   87
    Digital Petitions and Campaigns   89
    Creating Impactful Online Content   91
    Cybersecurity and Protecting Personal Data   92
    Building Online Communities   94

CHAPTER 10   98
Securing America's Future   98
    Fostering a Culture of Civic Engagement   98
    Educational Initiatives and Awareness Programs   100
    Proposing and Supporting Democratic Reforms   102
    Maintaining Vigilance and Ongoing Advocacy Efforts   103
    Leveraging Technology for Democracy   106

CONCLUSION   109

INTRODUCTION

What if the very foundations of American democracy were under threat, and the future of your rights depended on your awareness and action? As dramatic as it may sound, this is not a distant possibility but a pressing reality. Project 2025 represents a significant political shift with far-reaching implications for every citizen. This book serves as your indispensable guide to understanding these changes and taking meaningful steps to protect our democratic values.

Project 2025 matters now more than ever. In an age where misinformation can spread like wildfire and political polarization seems to deepen by the day, being informed is no longer just an option—it is a civic duty. The decisions made today will shape the democracy of tomorrow, and it is crucial that every citizen understands what is at stake. This is not merely a political issue but a fundamental aspect of our daily lives. From the laws governing our privacy to the policies affecting our healthcare, the impacts of Project 2025 extend far beyond the confines of Capitol Hill.

In light of these urgent issues, this book offers a thorough examination of Project 2025, aiming to demystify its proposals and provide clear insights into its potential consequences. Whether you are a concerned citizen alarmed by current political shifts, an activist looking to drive change, an educator seeking reliable resources, or a political professional needing detailed analysis, this book is designed to meet your needs. You will find comprehensive overviews, expert opinions, and actionable strategies to help you navigate this complex landscape.

At its core, this book seeks to empower you with the knowledge and tools necessary to engage meaningfully in the civic process. We delve into the origins and objectives of Project 2025, exploring how it came to be and why it holds such significance. Through meticulous research and analysis, we break down each aspect of the project, offering clear explanations and critical perspectives. By the end of this book, you will have a well-rounded understanding of the political climate and the ability to make informed decisions.

But this journey is not just about gaining knowledge; it is also about taking action. Understanding the intricacies of Project 2025 is only the first step. The real challenge lies in translating that understanding into active participation. Democracy is not a spectator sport; it thrives on the involvement of its citizens. This book emphasizes the importance of proactive engagement and provides practical guidance on how to get involved. From contacting your representatives to participating in local initiatives, there are numerous ways to make your voice heard.

We recognize that this can be daunting. The political arena can often seem inaccessible and overwhelming, but your contribution is invaluable. Every action, no matter how small, contributes to the larger goal of preserving our democratic values. This book aims to equip you with the confidence and skills needed to advocate effectively. Whether you are organizing a grassroots campaign or simply having informed discussions with friends and family, your efforts matter.

Moreover, collaboration is key. The challenges we face cannot be addressed in isolation. This book encourages readers to foster collaborative efforts for political reform. By working together, concerned citizens, activists, educators, and political professionals can create a powerful collective force for change. Throughout the chapters, we highlight examples of successful collaborations and offer insights into building strong networks and alliances. The spirit of cooperation and shared purpose can amplify the impact of individual actions, leading to more substantial and lasting reforms.

As we embark on this journey together, it is essential to keep an open mind and remain receptive to diverse perspectives. The beauty of democracy lies in its plurality of voices and ideas. While Project 2025 may present its own set of challenges, it also offers opportunities for growth and improvement. By engaging with this book, you are taking a vital step toward understanding and shaping the future of our democracy.

This introduction is just the beginning. What follows is a detailed exploration of Project 2025, designed to inform, inspire, and mobilize. Each chapter builds upon the previous one, creating a cohesive narrative that encapsulates the complexities and nuances of the political landscape. You will gain insights from experts in the field, real-life case studies, and practical advice, all aimed at empowering you to make a difference.

The road ahead may be filled with uncertainties, but with knowledge and determination, we can navigate these challenges. This book is your call to action—a rallying cry for all who cherish democracy and wish to see it flourish. Your awareness and engagement are crucial in shaping a future that upholds the values of freedom, equality, and justice.

So, let us take this journey together. Let us explore, understand, and act. The stakes are high, but so are the rewards. By staying informed and proactive, we can play our part in safeguarding the democratic principles that form the bedrock of our society. Welcome to your guide to Project 2025—a beacon of clarity in turbulent times and a roadmap to active citizenship.

CHAPTER 1

Understanding Project 2025

Understanding Project 2025 provides an in-depth analysis of the socio-political changes proposed by this ambitious initiative. The chapter delves into the framework and principles that drive Project 2025, highlighting its core focus on enhancing transparency, inclusivity, and civic engagement within American democratic structures. By addressing contemporary challenges through systemic changes grounded in democratic values, the project aims to reimagine and revitalize the current political landscape.

This chapter will explore the key components of Project 2025 designed to foster a more participatory and informed citizenry. It will examine mechanisms for improving public access to information, promoting equitable representation, and strengthening institutional accountability. The discussion will also cover the project's emphasis on civic education and awareness, along with proposals for direct democracy tools such as referendums and citizen assemblies. Additionally, the chapter will highlight the crucial role of strategic partnerships and technology in facilitating civic engagement and mobilizing collective action. Through these elements, readers will gain a comprehensive understanding of how Project 2025 seeks to bridge gaps in the socio-political landscape and drive significant democratic reforms.

Introduction to the Key Components of Project 2025

Project 2025 represents a comprehensive effort aimed at reimagining the socio-political structures of American democracy. Central to understanding this initiative involves a thorough grasp of its framework and principles. At its core, Project 2025 seeks to address contemporary challenges by proposing systemic changes grounded in democratic values. The project outlines a vision for ensuring greater transparency, inclusivity, and civic engagement in the political process.

The overall framework of Project 2025 includes several key components designed to foster a more participatory and informed citizenry. These components emphasize enhancing public access to information, promoting equitable representation, and strengthening institutional accountability. By prioritizing these elements, the initiative aims to bridge gaps in the current socio-political landscape, thereby revitalizing democratic processes.

Understanding the foundational tenets of Project 2025 is crucial for critically engaging with its proposals. One of the primary principles is the emphasis on civic education and awareness. The project underscores the importance of educating citizens about their rights, responsibilities, and the functioning of democratic institutions. This educational push is intended to empower individuals to participate more actively in the political discourse and decision-making processes.

Moreover, Project 2025 advocates for mechanisms that promote direct democracy, such as referendums and citizen assemblies. These tools are proposed to give the public a more substantial role in shaping policies that impact their lives. By incorporating elements of direct democracy, the initiative seeks to mitigate feelings of disenfranchisement and increase public trust in governmental actions.

An informed citizenry has a profound impact on political discourse. When people are knowledgeable about the issues at hand, they can engage in more meaningful and constructive debates. This leads to a more dynamic and responsive political environment where diverse viewpoints are acknowledged and respected. Project 2025's focus on civic education aims to cultivate a populace capable of critical thinking and informed decision-making, which are essential for a thriving democracy.

In addition to fostering informed discussions, an educated citizenry can hold elected officials accountable more effectively. When voters understand the implications of policy decisions and are aware of their leaders' actions, they can make better-informed choices at the ballot box. This heightened level of scrutiny ensures that politicians remain answerable to the people they serve, thus enhancing the integrity of the democratic system.

The clarity of Project 2025's goals and proposals is paramount in mobilizing collective action. Clear and concise communication of the project's objectives allows citizens to easily grasp what is at stake and why their involvement matters. Without this clarity, there is a risk of misunderstanding or apathy, both of which can undermine efforts to drive meaningful change.

Effective mobilization requires a shared understanding of the issues and a collective commitment to addressing them. Project 2025's emphasis on transparency and open dialogue aims to build consensus among various stakeholders, including concerned citizens, activists, educators, and political professionals. By fostering a common vision, the initiative seeks to galvanize diverse groups toward collective action.

Moreover, the project emphasizes the importance of strategic partnerships and alliances. Collaboration between different organizations and community groups can amplify the impact of advocacy efforts and create a more unified front. Project 2025 encourages the formation of coalitions that leverage each group's strengths to push for reforms that align with democratic values.

For example, partnerships between educational institutions and advocacy groups can enhance civic education programs, making them more accessible and impactful. Similarly, collaboration between grassroots organizations and think tanks can provide valuable insights and resources to bolster campaign strategies. By working together, these entities can create a more informed and engaged populace capable of driving substantial democratic reforms.

Project 2025 also recognizes the role of technology in facilitating civic engagement. Digital platforms offer innovative ways to disseminate information, rally support, and coordinate actions. The project advocates for leveraging these tools to reach a broader audience and streamline mobilization efforts. However, it also stresses the need for digital literacy to ensure that all citizens can navigate and utilize these platforms effectively.

Goals of the Initiative

Understanding the objectives of Project 2025 involves recognizing several critical elements that shape its proposed socio-political changes. These changes aim to address various facets of democratic governance and seek to realign values within a rapidly evolving political landscape.

First, identifying the goals of Project 2025 is essential to grasp the stakes involved. The project aims to introduce reforms that enhance transparency in governmental processes, increase civic participation, and promote a more equitable distribution of resources. By delineating these objectives, citizens can better understand how their daily lives might be impacted. For instance, increased transparency could lead to greater accountability among public officials, fostering trust and mitigating corruption. Additionally, promoting civic participation ensures that diverse voices are heard, leading to policies that more accurately reflect the will of the people.

Next, it's vital to engage in personal reflection on values and priorities within a democratic system. This introspection helps individuals recognize what they truly value in their society and what they wish to preserve or change. Democracy thrives on the alignment of its citizens' values with its governing principles. For example, if a community values social equity, they may support initiatives within Project 2025 that aim to reduce income inequality and provide broader access to education and healthcare. Reflecting on these values helps individuals decide where they stand on issues and how they might advocate for or against certain proposals.

Monitoring progress is another crucial objective within Project 2025. Without effective oversight, even the best-intentioned initiatives can falter. Establishing clear metrics and regular assessments to track the implementation of reforms ensures that goals are being met and allows for adjustments when necessary. For example, assessing the impact of a new policy on education access could involve tracking enrollment rates and student performance over time. This data-driven approach allows for the identification of successes and areas needing improvement, ensuring that resources are utilized effectively.

Encouraging civic engagement forms the backbone of Project 2025. Active participation from citizens not only legitimizes the democratic process but also enriches the political dialogue with diverse perspectives. Civic engagement can take many forms, from voting and participating in public forums to becoming involved in local governance or grassroots movements. When citizens are engaged, they are more likely to hold their representatives accountable and advocate for changes that benefit their communities. This active participation fosters a sense of ownership and responsibility towards societal outcomes, strengthening the democratic fabric.

To illustrate the importance of identifying goals, consider the example of a community-driven initiative to improve public transportation. By clearly defining the objective—such as reducing commute times and increasing accessibility for underserved areas—the community can mobilize resources and measure success based on specific criteria. This clarity helps align efforts and maintain focus on achieving the desired outcome.

Personal reflection on democratic values can be exemplified by examining debates around environmental policies. Individuals who prioritize sustainability may support laws aimed at reducing carbon emissions and protecting natural resources. Conversely, those who prioritize economic growth might advocate for policies that balance environmental concerns with business interests. Understanding one's values in this context allows for more informed and meaningful participation in the political process.

The necessity for monitoring progress can be seen in various public health initiatives. Programs aimed at improving public health outcomes often set specific targets, such as vaccination rates or the prevalence of certain diseases. Regular monitoring and reporting ensure these programs remain on track and can adapt to emerging challenges. This continuous evaluation process is key to achieving long-term success.

Encouragement for civic engagement is perhaps best highlighted by the role of social media in modern politics. Platforms like Twitter and Facebook have become powerful tools for mobilizing support, sharing information, and organizing events. Citizens who actively use these platforms can amplify their voices and connect with like-minded individuals, creating a robust network of engaged and informed participants. This digital dimension of civic engagement complements traditional methods and expands opportunities for involvement.

Overall, understanding the objectives of Project 2025 requires a multi-faceted approach that includes goal identification, personal reflection on democratic values, diligent monitoring of progress, and fostering civic engagement. Each element supports the others, creating a comprehensive framework for implementing and sustaining meaningful reforms. By focusing on these interconnected objectives, Project 2025 aims to create a more transparent, participatory, and equitable democratic system that reflects the collective aspirations of its citizens.

To ensure the successful realization of these objectives, it is imperative to foster an environment where open dialogue and collaboration are encouraged. This entails creating spaces for discussion and debate, whether through town hall meetings, public forums, or online platforms. By providing opportunities for citizens to voice their opinions and concerns, policymakers can gain valuable insights and build consensus around proposed changes.

Furthermore, education plays a pivotal role in empowering citizens to engage with the objectives of Project 2025. Educators and institutions can provide resources and learning opportunities that deepen understanding of democratic principles and the specific reforms being proposed. By fostering an informed citizenry, education contributes to more thoughtful and effective civic participation.

Historical Context and Background

The political landscape is never static; it shifts and transforms, often reflecting broader societal changes. To appreciate the proposals of Project 2025, it is essential to understand the historical evolution of political ideologies that have shaped contemporary policies. The trajectory from traditional political paradigms to more modern ideologies provides a context for the changes proposed by Project 2025.

Tracing historical shifts in political ideologies reveals a continuous evolution influenced by significant events and intellectual movements. In the early 20th century, political ideologies were largely defined by the conflict between liberal democracy and authoritarian regimes, such as fascism and communism. The aftermath of World War II saw the rise of liberal internationalism, which emphasized global cooperation and the spread of democratic governance. This era fostered economic prosperity and geopolitical stability for many Western countries.

As time progressed, the 1960s brought about a wave of social movements advocating for civil rights, gender equality, and environmental conservation. These movements challenged existing power structures and broadened the scope of political discourse. The subsequent decades saw the rise of neoliberalism, characterized by a focus on free-market policies, deregulation, and privatization. This shift was marked by influential leaders like Ronald Reagan in the United States and Margaret Thatcher in the United Kingdom.

Linking past events to the development of Project 2025 requires understanding how these ideological shifts influence contemporary politics. The neoliberal wave inspired a renewed emphasis on individual freedoms and market-driven solutions, shaping policy decisions into the early 21st century. However, the global financial crisis of 2008 exposed vulnerabilities in this model, prompting a re-evaluation of economic and social policies.

In response, there has been a resurgence of populist and nationalist movements, driven by perceived failures of globalism and economic inequality. These movements often challenge established political elites, advocating for more direct representation and protection of national interests. Project 2025 emerges within this context, proposing reforms aimed at addressing systemic issues highlighted by recent socio-political trends.

Analyzing factors contributing to political polarization is imperative to understand the divisive reactions to Project 2025. Over the past several decades, political discourse has become increasingly fragmented, with media consumption playing a significant role in amplifying ideological divides. The advent of social media has further entrenched echo chambers, where individuals are exposed primarily to viewpoints that reinforce their own beliefs. This phenomenon exacerbates misunderstandings and reduces opportunities for constructive dialogue.

Additionally, economic disparities and demographic shifts have fueled resentment and mistrust among different segments of society. Rural-urban divides, racial and ethnic tensions, and generational gaps contribute to a polarized political environment. These divisions make consensus-building challenging, complicating efforts to implement comprehensive reforms like those proposed in Project 2025.

Lessons from previous major political initiatives provide valuable insights into the potential challenges and strategies for implementing Project 2025. Historical examples highlight the complex interplay between change and resistance. For instance, the New Deal programs of the 1930s, introduced by President Franklin D. Roosevelt, faced significant opposition from business interests and conservative politicians. Despite this, the New Deal ultimately reshaped American society by establishing social safety nets and regulatory frameworks that persist to this day.

Similarly, the Civil Rights Movement of the 1950s and 1960s encountered fierce resistance but succeeded in dismantling institutionalized segregation and expanding civil liberties. These examples underscore the importance of persistent advocacy, coalition-building, and strategic compromises in achieving meaningful political change.

Project 2025 must navigate a landscape where both historical precedents and contemporary challenges intersect. By learning from past initiatives, proponents can develop strategies to address potential resistance and build broad-based support. This might involve engaging diverse stakeholders, fostering transparent communication, and emphasizing the long-term benefits of proposed reforms.

Primary Stakeholders and Their Motivations

The socio-political landscape of Project 2025 is shaped by a variety of stakeholders, each with distinct vested interests. Understanding these key players and their motivations is essential for comprehending the broader implications of the initiative.

Political figures and organizations are at the forefront of advocating for Project 2025. High-profile politicians, including influential senators and representatives, have lent their support to the movement. Their backing often stems from ideological alignment with the project's principles, which aim to reshape governance and policy frameworks in line with evolving societal needs. Key political organizations, such as prominent think tanks and advocacy groups, have also played a significant role. These entities provide intellectual underpinning and strategic direction, utilizing research and policy proposals to shape public opinion and legislative agendas.

Economic motivators further illuminate the reasons behind stakeholder support for Project 2025. Various industries and business leaders perceive potential economic benefits, ranging from deregulation to favorable tax policies. By aligning themselves with the project, they hope to influence policy outcomes that could lead to increased profitability and market expansion. The tech sector, for instance, sees opportunities in proposed changes to data privacy laws and digital infrastructure investments. Similarly, traditional industries like manufacturing anticipate gains from revised trade agreements and labor regulations. The promise of economic growth and competitive advantage thus drives substantial support from corporate stakeholders.

The endorsement of Project 2025 is also bolstered by social movements and cultural narratives. A range of grassroots organizations and civic groups, drawn together by shared values and goals, champion the initiative. These movements often frame their support in terms of enhancing democratic participation, promoting social justice, and addressing long-standing inequalities. Cultural narratives play a crucial role in sustaining momentum, as they resonate with the broader public and create a sense of collective purpose. Whether through rallies, social media campaigns, or community outreach, these groups mobilize citizens and amplify their voices, ensuring that the project's vision aligns with popular aspirations.

However, it is important to recognize that not all stakeholders are in favor of Project 2025. Various groups have emerged in opposition, citing concerns about its potential impact. Political opponents argue that the project may concentrate power and undermine checks and balances within the government. They worry that sweeping changes could erode foundational democratic principles and lead to unintended consequences. Economically, some sectors fear that new policies might disrupt established markets and impose burdensome regulations. Small businesses, in particular, express apprehension about competing with larger corporations that stand to benefit disproportionately.

Additionally, social resistance to Project 2025 is evident among those who believe the initiative fails to address critical issues such as climate change, racial justice, and workers' rights. These critics argue that the project's focus on economic growth may overshadow pressing environmental and social challenges. Activists and advocacy groups actively campaign against the aspects they find detrimental, organizing protests, drafting petitions, and engaging in public discourse to highlight their dissenting perspectives.

Given the complexity of these dynamics, comprehending the breadth of stakeholder interests necessitates an exploration of civic responses and mobilization efforts. Concerned citizens and advocacy networks take proactive measures to engage with Project 2025, both in support and opposition. Civic engagement manifests in various forms, including town hall meetings, lobbying efforts, and public forums where individuals can voice their opinions and collaborate on strategies. These spaces facilitate dialogue and foster a sense of agency among participants, enabling them to influence decision-making processes.

Supporters of Project 2025 utilize civic mobilization to build coalitions and strengthen their advocacy. By coordinating with like-minded groups and leveraging technological platforms, they maximize their reach and impact. Educational programs, workshops, and informational campaigns are organized to inform the public about the project's goals and benefits, encouraging active participation in shaping its trajectory.

Conversely, opponents leverage similar tactics to galvanize resistance. They organize awareness campaigns aimed at highlighting perceived flaws and risks associated with the initiative. Public debates are held, featuring experts and activists who provide alternative viewpoints and challenge prevailing narratives. These efforts aim to foster critical thinking and compel policymakers to consider diverse perspectives when deliberating on Project 2025.

Initial Reactions and Controversies Surrounding the Proposal

Immediate Responses and Controversies Following the Announcement of Project 2025

The announcement of Project 2025 set off a wave of immediate responses and controversies across various sectors of society. Understanding these reactions provides insight into the socio-political landscape and the contentious nature of the proposals put forth.

Public reactions to Project 2025 were polarized, with clear divisions between supporters and opponents. On one side, proponents hailed the initiative as a necessary step toward modernizing governance and addressing contemporary challenges. They argued that the changes proposed would enhance efficiency, accountability, and responsiveness within governmental institutions. Many supporters came from diverse backgrounds; some were driven by a desire for more transparent governance, while others viewed the reforms as a means to dismantle long-standing bureaucratic obstacles.

On the other hand, a significant portion of the public expressed strong opposition. Critics voiced concerns over potential threats to democratic values and the concentration of power. They feared that the proposed changes could lead to authoritarian tendencies or undermine existing checks and balances. These opponents often included civil rights activists, political analysts, and ordinary citizens worried about preserving democratic integrity.

Media coverage played a pivotal role in shaping public perception of Project 2025. News outlets and social media platforms offered varying narratives, amplifying the division in public opinion. Supportive media sources framed the project as a forward-thinking blueprint for the future, emphasizing its potential benefits. Articles and reports highlighted success stories from other countries that had implemented similar reforms, painting an optimistic picture of what Project 2025 could achieve.

Conversely, oppositional media focused on the risks and drawbacks, scrutinizing every aspect of the proposals. Investigative journalism uncovered potential conflicts of interest and questioned the intentions behind certain reforms. Editorials and opinion pieces warned readers about potential erosions of freedoms and democratic principles. This duality in coverage fostered an environment where individuals' pre-existing beliefs were reinforced, leading to further polarization.

Scholarly critiques and endorsements provided yet another layer of complexity to the discourse surrounding Project 2025. Academic experts from various fields, including political science, economics, and law, weighed in on the proposals. Supportive scholars highlighted the innovative aspects of the project, arguing that it represented a bold attempt to address systemic issues. They provided evidence from empirical studies and theoretical frameworks to substantiate their claims.

However, there was no shortage of academic dissent. Critics from the scholarly community raised alarm bells about potential negative consequences. They pointed to historical examples where similar reforms had led to unintended outcomes, cautioning against hasty implementation. Scholarly articles delved into the nuances of the proposed changes, examining their potential impact on different segments of society. These critiques often called for a more gradual, measured approach to reform.

In analyzing the overall response to Project 2025, it is crucial to consider the role of civic mobilization. Grassroots movements and community organizations emerged as significant players in shaping political outcomes. Protests, petitions, and public forums became common tools for expressing dissent or support. These collective actions demonstrated the power of community mobilization in influencing policy decisions. Advocacy groups rallied their members to engage in informed discussions, lobby decision-makers, and participate in civic activities.

Examples of effective civic mobilization abound. In several cities, local activists organized town hall meetings, inviting policymakers to discuss the implications of Project 2025 with constituents. These events provided a platform for open dialogue, allowing citizens to voice their concerns and ask pertinent questions. Additionally, social media campaigns helped amplify the reach of grassroots efforts, connecting like-minded individuals and fostering a sense of solidarity.

Throughout this chapter, we have explored the comprehensive socio-political changes proposed by Project 2025, focusing on enhancing transparency, inclusivity, and civic engagement within democratic processes. The initiative emphasizes civic education, direct democracy mechanisms, strategic partnerships, and leveraging technology to create an informed and participatory citizenry. These proposals aim to address contemporary challenges by fostering a more equitable, accountable, and responsive political environment.

As we reflect on the key components of Project 2025, it becomes clear that its success hinges on collective efforts and ongoing dialogue among various stakeholders, including citizens, educators, activists, and political professionals. By understanding the principles and goals outlined in this chapter, we can better appreciate the project's potential to transform governance and inspire meaningful reforms. Moving forward, it will be crucial to maintain open communication, monitor progress diligently, and encourage active participation to ensure that the vision of Project 2025 is realized effectively.

CHAPTER 2

The Blueprint: Legislative and Social Changes

Legislative and social changes are critical components in shaping the future of American democracy under Project 2025. This chapter delves into these proposed reforms, examining how they could transform various aspects of governance and civil rights in the United States. The analysis begins by exploring key legislative reforms, such as modifications to voting laws aimed at addressing voter fraud. However, these changes may also impact voter access and engagement, particularly within marginalized communities. Additionally, significant shifts in regulatory policies across sectors like healthcare, environmental regulation, and labor laws are scrutinized for their potential effects on public welfare and individual rights.

The chapter further extends its analysis to the broader implications of these legislative changes, highlighting the proposed amendments to the U.S. Constitution and their possible ramifications for personal liberties. New enforcement mechanisms designed to ensure compliance with these legislative changes are also discussed, emphasizing both the intended benefits and the risks associated with increased surveillance and punitive actions. By evaluating the multifaceted impacts of Project 2025's reforms, this chapter aims to provide a comprehensive understanding of how these changes might shape the democratic principles and everyday lives of American citizens.

Key Legislative Reforms Proposed

In exploring the legislative reforms proposed under Project 2025, it is essential to understand how these changes might alter governance and civil rights in the United States. The first area requiring examination involves proposed changes to voting laws. Under Project 2025, various modifications aim to address voter fraud but may simultaneously impact voter access. Increased barriers to registration, such as more stringent identification requirements or reduced availability of online registration options, could disproportionately affect marginalized communities. Additionally, enhanced scrutiny of mail-in ballots, through measures like stricter verification processes or limiting the reasons one can vote by mail, may disenfranchise voters who rely on this method for convenience or necessity.

These proposed changes could lead to significant shifts in voter turnout and engagement. For instance, more rigorous ID requirements have been shown in some studies to reduce participation among groups less likely to possess government-issued identification, including low-income individuals and racial minorities. Furthermore, limiting mail-in voting access could pose challenges for older adults, people with disabilities, and those living in remote areas. Such barriers threaten to undermine the democratic principle of equal access to the ballot box, potentially skewing electoral outcomes in favor of those able to navigate these restrictions more easily.

Moving on from voting laws, Project 2025 also proposes substantial shifts in regulatory policies affecting various sectors. In healthcare, deregulatory measures could result in fewer protections for patients and increased power for insurance companies and private healthcare providers. Changes to environmental regulations might prioritize economic growth over sustainability, leading to relaxed standards on pollutants, which could have dire consequences for public health and climate change efforts. Labor laws are another critical area; potential impacts include weakening union powers and dismantling worker protections, such as minimum wage laws and safety regulations.

Considering healthcare deregulation, the implications could be wide-ranging. Reduced oversight might accelerate the privatization of healthcare, making access dependent on one's ability to pay rather than need. This could exacerbate existing disparities in health outcomes, particularly among low-income populations and minorities who already face significant barriers to quality care. In the realm of environmental regulation, scaling back rules designed to limit emissions and protect natural resources could lead to short-term economic benefits but long-term environmental degradation, affecting air and water quality and contributing to global climate challenges.

Labor law changes proposed under Project 2025 could transform the working landscape significantly. Reducing the power of unions, for example, might weaken collective bargaining efforts that secure fair wages and safe working conditions. Without these protections, workers could face increased exploitation, reduced compensation, and greater occupational hazards. Deregulation in these sectors aligns with a broader agenda prioritizing corporate interests and economic flexibility over social welfare and workers' rights.

Another crucial aspect of Project 2025 involves proposed amendments to the U.S. Constitution. These amendments could solidify enduring partisan divides and potentially infringe upon personal liberties. For instance, propositions to amend the Constitution might include redefining citizenship, altering the balance of powers between federal and state governments, or changing fundamental rights related to privacy, free speech, or due process. Such changes would not only foster partisan entrenchment but also risk reversing decades of progress in expanding civil liberties and protecting individual freedoms.

Constitutional amendments introduced under Project 2025 merit careful scrutiny. By altering foundational legal frameworks, they could create precedents challenging to reverse. If citizenship criteria are restricted, for example, millions of immigrants could find their status jeopardized, facing heightened uncertainty and decreased protection under the law. Reallocating powers between federal and state entities might lead to inconsistent application of rights and protections across states, exacerbating regional inequalities and creating confusion about citizens' rights. Changes to privacy and free speech rights could open the door to increased government surveillance and censorship, threatening the democratic ideals of freedom and autonomy.

Finally, it is important to consider the mechanisms proposed to enforce these legislative changes. Project 2025 outlines the creation of new bodies dedicated to overseeing compliance, surveillance, and control. While these mechanisms are intended to ensure adherence to new laws, they raise significant concerns about privacy and civil liberties. Enhanced surveillance measures, for example, might involve expanded use of data tracking, facial recognition technology, and other monitoring tools. Control models could prioritize punitive actions over constructive engagement, focusing on detecting and punishing non-compliance rather than fostering understanding and cooperation.

The establishment of these enforcement bodies presents numerous ethical and practical dilemmas. Expanding surveillance capabilities without robust oversight could lead to abuses of power and violations of privacy. Initiatives aimed at increasing governmental control and monitoring may deter lawful dissent and stifle political activism, undermining fundamental democratic principles. Surveillance methods like data tracking and facial recognition are often fraught with biases, particularly against minority communities, further marginalizing vulnerable populations and eroding public trust in government institutions.

Impact on Social Policies and Public Welfare

Project 2025 proposes several significant legislative and social changes that could reshape the landscape of American democracy and citizens' rights. This section focuses on evaluating how these proposed changes could affect social policies and essential public welfare programs, detailing potential modifications, impacts on healthcare and education, and shifts in social justice initiatives.

First, it is crucial to understand how Project 2025 may modify existing welfare programs. These programs are fundamental to supporting vulnerable populations, providing financial aid, food assistance, and housing support. One of the most concerning aspects is the potential reduction of benefits. For instance, benefits from programs such as the Supplemental Nutrition Assistance Program (SNAP) could be scaled back, which would directly impact millions of low-income families who rely on this aid to meet their basic nutritional needs.

Moreover, changes to eligibility criteria could further restrict access to these vital services. Currently, many welfare programs base eligibility on income thresholds and family size, among other factors. Under Project 2025, stricter criteria might be introduced, potentially disenfranchising individuals who are on the cusp of qualifying. This tightening of requirements can lead to increased poverty rates and greater disparity between socio-economic classes.

Healthcare policy is another area likely to be significantly impacted by Project 2025. Rollbacks in public healthcare options are a point of concern. Public health insurance programs like Medicaid provide coverage to millions of Americans, especially those with low incomes or disabilities. Changes under Project 2025 might lead to reduced funding for Medicaid, thereby limiting the scope and quality of healthcare services available to beneficiaries.

Additionally, alterations to Medicaid's structure could include shifting more responsibilities to state governments, which might not have the resources to maintain the current level of service. Such rollbacks could lead to fewer people receiving necessary medical care, increased out-of-pocket costs, and higher overall health disparities. Furthermore, the push towards privatization of healthcare services may result in a system where profit motives overshadow patient care, reducing the accessibility and affordability of healthcare for many.

When exploring the potential impacts on educational policies, one cannot ignore the possible budget cuts to public education. Public schools across the United States already face funding challenges, and further reductions could exacerbate existing issues. Budget cuts could lead to larger class sizes, reduced extracurricular activities, and diminished support services such as special education and counseling. This could adversely affect students' overall learning experiences and outcomes, particularly in underfunded districts.

Shifts towards privatized education are also part of the proposed changes. While some argue that privatization introduces healthy competition and innovation, it often comes at the cost of equity. Private institutions may prioritize admissions based on academic performance or financial capability, leaving behind students who do not meet these criteria. This shift could widen the gap between privileged and underprivileged students, undermining the principle of equal opportunity in education.

Lastly, it is imperative to discuss the proposed changes to social justice efforts. Future legislation under Project 2025 could potentially roll back gains made in LGBTQ+ and minority rights. Over recent decades, there have been significant strides towards achieving equality and justice for marginalized communities. However, the proposed legislative changes could reverse these advancements, affecting anti-discrimination laws, marriage equality, and protections against hate crimes. For example, amendments to civil rights legislation could reduce the legal recourses available to individuals facing discrimination based on sexual orientation or gender identity.

Rollback in minority rights could also manifest through new voter suppression laws, gerrymandering, and limited representation in political processes. These measures would disproportionately affect communities of color, undermining their ability to participate fully in democratic governance.

Future Implications for Healthcare and Education

Project 2025 proposes significant changes that aim to reshape healthcare and education in America. A deep dive into these areas reveals the profound and potentially lasting implications on societal structures and individual lives. Understanding these shifts is critical for grasping the broader impact of Project 2025.

The anticipated shifts in healthcare delivery frameworks form a crucial part of this assessment. One of the most significant potential changes is the move towards increased privatization of healthcare services. This shift could fundamentally alter the healthcare landscape, making access to quality care more dependent on an individual's financial capacity. Privatization may lead to a two-tier system where those with means receive timely and comprehensive care while others face longer wait times and limited options. The emphasis might shift from preventive care to emergency care, increasing strain on emergency services and possibly leading to higher overall healthcare costs.

Beyond privatization, another critical aspect to consider is the potential redirection of funds towards emergency care. While improving emergency response capabilities can undoubtedly save lives, it might also result in the neglect of essential preventative and chronic care services. Preventive measures, including routine screenings and vaccinations, are vital for maintaining public health and can reduce the long-term burden on emergency services. If these areas suffer due to funding reallocations, there might be an increase in preventable diseases and complications, which could further inflate healthcare costs and worsen health outcomes for many citizens.

Turning to education, the future of educational equity and access under Project 2025 looks particularly concerning. Diminished public school funding is a central issue, as reduced financial support can have cascading effects on the quality of education provided. Schools may struggle to maintain infrastructure, hire qualified teachers, and provide necessary resources such as textbooks and technology. This shortfall disproportionately affects lower-income districts, exacerbating existing disparities and limiting opportunities for students who rely most heavily on public education.

Moreover, Project 2025's increased reliance on standardized testing raises several issues. While standardized tests can offer metrics for evaluating student performance and school efficiency, an overemphasis on testing can narrow the curriculum, stifling creativity and critical thinking. Teachers may feel pressured to "teach to the test," focusing primarily on test-taking skills rather than providing a well-rounded education. This trend can undermine efforts to foster holistic development and limit students' preparedness for real-world challenges beyond standardized assessments.

Community-based health initiatives form another critical layer of the discussion. These grassroots health programs play an essential role in addressing local health needs, promoting wellness, and delivering culturally competent care. However, Project 2025's proposed changes include potential funding cuts and reduced support for such initiatives. This loss of funding could cripple programs that provide essential services like mental health support, nutrition education, and disease prevention campaigns. Community programs often fill gaps left by larger healthcare systems, so their reduction or elimination would likely undermine public health at the local level, disproportionately affecting vulnerable populations.

Analyzing the sustainability of these proposed systemic changes involves considering several factors: public acceptance, economic volatility, and ethical considerations. Public acceptance is critical; reforms that do not resonate with citizens may face resistance, reducing their effectiveness and longevity. Economic volatility also plays a significant role; during times of economic downturn, funding and resource allocation become even more challenging, potentially destabilizing new systems put in place under Project 2025. Encouragingly, there are historical precedents where public pushback has led to policy revisions, suggesting that active civic engagement can shape outcomes.

Ethical considerations are equally important. Healthcare and education are fundamental human rights, and any reform must prioritize equity and access. Policies that deepen inequalities or disproportionately affect marginalized communities raise serious ethical concerns. Policymakers must ensure that reforms align with principles of justice and inclusivity, creating systems that serve all citizens fairly.

Economic Impacts and Job Market Shifts

Projected Economic Changes and Potential Shifts in the Job Market under Project 2025

As we delve into the intricacies of Project 2025, it becomes necessary to evaluate its potential impact on the American economy and job market. This section aims to dissect the projected economic changes and shifts in employment opportunities that could arise as a consequence of this initiative.

Anticipated Shifts in Employment Opportunities

One of the most prominent factors driving changes in employment opportunities is the acceleration of automation and technological advancements. Automation has already begun to reshape various industries, from manufacturing to services, replacing numerous traditional jobs with automated systems. This trend is expected to continue and even intensify under Project 2025 as policies may facilitate and incentivize businesses to adopt new technologies at a faster pace.

The rise of the gig economy also plays a significant role in redefining employment landscapes. Gig work, characterized by short-term contracts and freelance tasks, offers flexibility but often lacks job security and benefits associated with traditional full-time employment. Project 2025 might encourage this shift further by promoting deregulation measures that make it easier for companies to hire gig workers while potentially reducing labor protections.

These transformations in the job market necessitate a closer examination of how workforce dynamics will evolve. For instance, roles requiring repetitive tasks are more likely to be automated, whereas positions necessitating creativity, critical thinking, and emotional intelligence may experience growth. The challenge lies in ensuring that workers displaced by automation can transition into these emerging roles through upskilling and reskilling initiatives.

Proposed Changes in Wage Policies and Labor Protections

Another critical consideration is the potential overhaul of wage policies and labor protections under Project 2025. One controversial proposal is the possible abolishment of minimum wage laws. Proponents argue that removing minimum wage requirements could stimulate job creation by enabling businesses to lower labor costs. However, this move could exacerbate income inequality and push more workers into low-paying, precarious jobs without essential benefits.

Additionally, limitations on union activities could significantly impact labor rights. Unions have historically been instrumental in securing better wages, benefits, and working conditions for their members. Restricting their influence might weaken collective bargaining power, leaving workers more vulnerable to exploitation. It is imperative to analyze how such changes would affect the balance of power between employers and employees and consider alternative mechanisms to protect workers' rights.

Furthermore, proposed alterations to overtime regulations and workplace safety standards must be scrutinized. Any reduction in these protections could lead to longer working hours without adequate compensation and increased risk of workplace injuries. A thorough evaluation of these policy changes is necessary to ensure they do not undermine the well-being and financial stability of American workers.

Macroeconomic Shifts Affecting Local Communities

On a broader scale, Project 2025 could trigger significant macroeconomic shifts that reverberate through local communities. One major concern is the growing competition from corporate monopolies. Large corporations, with their vast resources and economies of scale, can dominate markets, stifling competition and driving smaller businesses out. This concentration of economic power can result in fewer choices for consumers and diminished local entrepreneurship.

Changes to federal funding allocations also warrant attention. Project 2025 might prioritize certain sectors or regions for investment, leading to uneven economic development. While some areas could benefit from increased funding and job creation, others may experience resource divestment, exacerbating regional disparities. The reallocation of funds could impact essential public services such as education, healthcare, and infrastructure, further influencing the economic vitality of affected communities.

Moreover, shifts in trade policies and international relations under Project 2025 could have far-reaching implications. Tariff changes, trade agreements, and geopolitical tensions can influence global supply chains and export markets. Local economies dependent on specific industries, such as agriculture or manufacturing, might face disruptions that necessitate adaptation strategies.

Future Economic Challenges and Trends

Lastly, it is crucial to anticipate future economic challenges and trends resulting from Project 2025. Economic instability is a potential risk, particularly if rapid policy changes create uncertainty for businesses and investors. Fluctuations in market confidence can lead to volatility, affecting stock prices, capital flows, and consumer spending.

The long-term viability of policies introduced under Project 2025 must also be considered. While some measures may yield immediate benefits, their sustainability could be questionable. For example, tax cuts aimed at stimulating economic growth might initially boost consumption but lead to budget deficits and reduced public investment in the long run.

Another trend worth noting is the increasing importance of sustainability and environmental considerations in economic planning. As concerns about climate change and resource depletion grow, policies that promote green technologies and sustainable practices will likely gain traction. Project 2025's alignment with these goals could determine its success in fostering a resilient and inclusive economy.

New Enforcement Mechanisms

The Blueprint: Legislative and Social Changes

To ensure the legislative and social changes proposed under Project 2025 are effectively implemented, new mechanisms have been designed to oversee compliance. This section delves into these mechanisms, starting with the explanation of newly proposed bodies created specifically for this purpose. These bodies will play crucial roles in maintaining adherence to the outlined changes, each endowed with distinct responsibilities and powers.

One of the primary new entities proposed is the Compliance Oversight Bureau (COB). This body is envisioned to function as the central authority responsible for monitoring the implementation of legislative reforms. COB will have the power to conduct audits, enforce regulations, and issue penalties for non-compliance. Its scope extends to both public and private sectors, ensuring that various stakeholders adhere to the changes mandated under Project 2025. The establishment of COB aims to create a more structured approach to compliance, providing clear guidelines and expectations for all affected parties.

In addition to COB, regional enforcement agencies will be set up to manage local compliance. These agencies will report to COB but will have autonomy in handling region-specific issues. Their role includes conducting local inspections, addressing community concerns, and facilitating communication between the national bureau and local entities. This decentralized model is intended to make enforcement more flexible and responsive to the needs of different areas.

However, increased surveillance and control measures accompany these new oversight bodies, raising significant privacy concerns. Under Project 2025, the proposal includes enhanced surveillance systems to monitor compliance more closely. These measures involve advanced technologies such as widespread use of CCTV, digital tracking, and data collection from various sources including social media and financial transactions. While the intention behind these measures is to ensure thorough enforcement and prevent any circumvention of the new laws, they inevitably lead to potential intrusions into personal privacy.

Critics argue that such extensive surveillance could infringe upon individual freedoms and erode trust between citizens and the government. Privacy advocates highlight the risks of misuse or overreach, where collected data might be used beyond its original purpose, leading to unwarranted scrutiny and discrimination. To address these concerns, it is essential to incorporate strict data protection regulations and transparency in the implementation process. This includes clear definitions of what data can be collected, how it can be used, and the rights of individuals to access and correct their information.

Beyond surveillance, the enforcement models proposed lean heavily towards punitive actions rather than constructive engagement. This approach emphasizes penalties, fines, and legal repercussions for non-compliance, which can have significant impacts on local governance. For instance, municipalities might face stringent penalties for failing to implement certain aspects of the legislative changes, resulting in strained local budgets and resources.

This punitive model may foster an environment of fear and adversarial relationships between governing bodies and citizens. Instead of encouraging cooperation and voluntary compliance, a punitive focus can lead to resistance, hidden defiance, or superficial adherence without genuine commitment to the changes. Additionally, smaller communities with limited resources might struggle disproportionately under the weight of these enforcement measures, exacerbating existing inequalities.

Project 2025's reliance on punitive actions underscores the need for balanced enforcement strategies. Incorporating elements of education, support, and incentives alongside penalties could create a more holistic enforcement mechanism. Such an approach would encourage genuine adoption of reforms, fostering a collaborative relationship between authorities and citizens. It is crucial to consider these dynamics to avoid deepening divides and to promote sustainable, long-term compliance.

The broader implications of these enforcement mechanisms reach into the fabric of democratic processes and citizens' rights. Enhanced surveillance and aggressive enforcement can alter the relationship between individuals and the state, shifting it towards greater control and less personal freedom. A democracy thrives on the principles of trust, voluntary participation, and respect for individual liberties. When enforcement mechanisms undermine these principles, they threaten the core values of democratic governance.

For example, if citizens feel constantly monitored and fear reprisal for dissenting views, there is a chilling effect on free speech and civic engagement. People may become less willing to participate in political processes, voice opinions, or engage in activism, leading to a less vibrant and representative democratic society. Furthermore, the perception of an overly punitive state can erode trust in governmental institutions, making it harder to achieve collective goals and societal progress.

Moreover, when the balance tips too far towards surveillance and punishment, marginalized groups often bear the brunt of these measures. Historically disadvantaged communities might experience heightened scrutiny and disproportionately severe penalties, reinforcing systemic biases and injustices. To mitigate these risks, the enforcement mechanisms of Project 2025 must be implemented with equity and fairness at the forefront. This involves continuous assessment, community involvement, and mechanisms for redress and accountability.

Insights and Implications

In this chapter, we have explored the legislative and social changes proposed under Project 2025, focusing on their potential implications for American democracy and citizens' rights. The proposed modifications to voting laws, such as stricter identification requirements and limitations on mail-in ballots, raise significant concerns about voter access and participation. These changes could disproportionately impact marginalized communities, threatening the democratic principle of equal access to voting. Additionally, the deregulatory measures in healthcare, environmental policy, and labor laws present complex challenges. While aimed at promoting economic growth, these changes may reduce protections for vulnerable populations and exacerbate existing inequalities.

Moreover, the proposed constitutional amendments and new enforcement mechanisms warrant careful consideration. Changes to fundamental rights and governance structures could erode personal liberties and deepen partisan divides. Enhanced surveillance and punitive control models pose risks to privacy and civil liberties, potentially deterring civic engagement and stifling political dissent. It is essential for concerned citizens, activists, educators, and political professionals to critically assess these reforms to safeguard democratic values and ensure that policies promote inclusivity and fairness.

CHAPTER 3

Unpacking Potential Risks

Exploring the potential risks posed to democracy by Project 2025 invites a detailed examination of how these proposals could affect various democratic principles and systems. Individuals concerned with preserving individual freedoms, judicial integrity, and civil liberties will find this chapter compelling. It discusses the multifaceted ways in which Project 2025 might challenge these essential components of a democratic society.

This chapter delves into three primary areas: the erosion of civil liberties, challenges to judicial independence, and the broader impacts on free speech and press freedoms. Each section provides a close look at how specific proposals could lead to increased surveillance, restrictions on public assembly, cuts in legal aid, politicization of the judiciary, budget reductions for courts, and changes in judicial review standards. Additionally, it examines the potential discrimination within security measures and the wide-reaching consequences on marginalized communities. By scrutinizing these aspects, the chapter offers a comprehensive overview vital for activists, educators, political professionals, and concerned citizens aiming to safeguard democratic values against potential threats posed by Project 2025.

Erosion of Civil Liberties

The changes proposed by Project 2025 hold significant implications for individual freedoms and civil liberties. One of the most concerning aspects is the potential for increased surveillance justified by national security concerns. While the intention may be to safeguard the nation, such measures often lead to violations of privacy. Surveillance programs can become intrusive, monitoring personal communications, online activities, and even physical movements. This constant observation could stifle free expression as individuals may feel pressured to self-censor, fearing repercussions for voicing dissenting opinions.

Furthermore, historical examples show a pattern where increased surveillance has been used to target dissenting voices. During the Cold War era, the U.S. government conducted extensive surveillance on civil rights leaders and anti-war activists, labeling them as threats to national security. Similar practices could resurface under the guise of Project 2025, disproportionately affecting activists, journalists, and marginalized communities who often challenge the status quo. Such actions not only violate privacy but also undermine democratic principles by creating an atmosphere of fear and repression.

Another critical area of concern is the potential restrictions on public assembly. The right to assemble peacefully is a cornerstone of democracy, allowing citizens to express their views, protest against injustices, and advocate for change. However, Project 2025's proposals could impose stringent regulations on public gatherings, citing reasons such as maintaining public order or preventing violence. These restrictions could marginalize grassroots movements that rely on public demonstrations to amplify their voices. Historically, movements like the Civil Rights Movement and Women's Suffrage relied heavily on public assembly to effectuate change. Limiting this right could suppress social movements that champion equality and justice.

Moreover, these restrictions would disproportionately affect marginalized communities. Often, these communities organize and participate in public assemblies to highlight systemic inequalities and demand better treatment. Curtailing their ability to gather and protest would silence their grievances and perpetuate existing power imbalances. It is essential to recognize that policies restricting public assembly should be carefully scrutinized to ensure they do not infringe upon the fundamental rights of citizens.

Cuts in legal aid are another alarming proposal within Project 2025, which could profoundly impact vulnerable populations' access to justice. Legal aid services provide crucial support to those who cannot afford private legal representation. Reducing funding for these services would leave many without the necessary legal assistance to navigate the judicial system. Vulnerable groups, including low-income individuals, minorities, and immigrants, would be disproportionately affected, facing significant barriers to obtaining fair and timely justice.

Additionally, cuts in legal aid could shift the focus from rehabilitation to punitive measures. Without adequate legal support, individuals may face harsher penalties and lengthier incarcerations, perpetuating a cycle of punishment rather than rehabilitation. This approach overlooks the importance of addressing underlying issues such as poverty, addiction, and mental health, which often contribute to criminal behavior. A balanced justice system should prioritize rehabilitation and reintegration, providing individuals with opportunities to rebuild their lives and contribute positively to society.

Policies framed as security measures within Project 2025 also risk being discriminatory, deepening societal divisions, and targeting specific demographic groups. Security measures, while intended to protect, can sometimes be implemented in ways that disproportionately affect certain communities. For example, profiling based on race, ethnicity, or religion can lead to discriminatory practices, where individuals from specific groups are subjected to heightened scrutiny and suspicion.

This type of discrimination can erode trust between communities and law enforcement agencies, making it more challenging to foster collaboration and cooperation. Instead of enhancing security, such practices can fuel resentment and alienation, further dividing society. It is crucial for security policies to be inclusive and unbiased, ensuring that all individuals are treated fairly and equitably.

To illustrate, the post-9/11 era saw increased profiling and surveillance of Muslim communities under the pretext of combating terrorism. Many innocent individuals endured unwarranted scrutiny, leading to feelings of fear and alienation. Similar patterns could emerge with Project 2025, potentially targeting specific demographic groups and perpetuating cycles of discrimination and division. Effective security policies should balance national safety with the protection of civil liberties, fostering a sense of unity and mutual respect among diverse communities.

Challenges to Judicial Independence

The integrity and autonomy of the judiciary are crucial pillars of any democratic society. Project 2025, with its sweeping reforms, poses several potential risks to these foundational elements. One significant risk is the increased politicization in the selection of judges. By emphasizing political loyalty over judicial qualifications, this approach could erode public trust in the judiciary's impartiality. Judges are expected to interpret laws without partisan bias. However, if they are perceived as extensions of political parties, the public may question their rulings, undermining confidence in the entire judicial system. This scenario sets a dangerous precedent where future administrations might feel justified in exerting undue influence over judicial appointments.

Moreover, budget reductions for court systems under Project 2025 could hinder their ability to function effectively. Courts require adequate funding to manage caseloads, support staff, and maintain infrastructure. Budget cuts can lead to delays in legal proceedings, denying timely justice. Marginalized communities, who often rely on public defenders and legal aid, would be disproportionately affected. Delayed justice isn't just an inconvenience; it can result in prolonged detentions for those unable to afford bail or legal representation, exacerbating existing inequalities within the justice system.

Project 2025 also proposes changes in judicial review standards, which could tilt rulings in favor of governmental authority. Judicial review serves as a check on executive and legislative powers by ensuring that laws and policies comply with constitutional provisions. Alterations in these standards threaten to undermine established precedents and legal protections for voter and civil rights. For instance, reducing the judiciary's ability to challenge gerrymandering or voter suppression laws could disenfranchise significant portions of the electorate, weakening the very foundation of democratic participation.

Furthermore, public perception manipulation campaigns pose another grave threat to the judiciary under Project 2025. These campaigns aim to delegitimize the court system, eroding trust in its decisions and independence. A common tactic involves discrediting judges by portraying them as biased or corrupt when their rulings are unfavorable to certain political agendas. This erosion of trust disrupts the balance of power fundamental to democracy. If the public views the judiciary as merely another political tool rather than an independent arbiter of justice, the legitimacy of its rulings comes into question, threatening the rule of law.

Taken together, these aspects highlight the multifaceted nature of the risks posed by Project 2025 to the judiciary's integrity and autonomy. Increased politicization in judge selection not only diminishes public trust but also signals to future administrations that judicial appointments are fair game for political maneuvering. The repercussions are profound, leading to a judiciary less focused on legal merits and more on political affiliations.

Budget cuts further complicate the functioning of courts, introducing inefficiencies that stall justice. Particularly for marginalized communities, such delays can have dire consequences. Access to justice should be equitable, but underfunded courts create an environment where only the affluent can navigate the legal system swiftly and effectively. This diverges starkly from the democratic ideal of equal treatment under the law.

Changes in judicial review standards present a subtler yet equally concerning danger. By narrowing the scope of judicial oversight, these reforms could enable governmental overreach. Historical examples demonstrate how pivotal judicial reviews have been in safeguarding rights and liberties. Any dilution of this process risks curtailing essential checks and balances, emboldening executive and legislative branches at the expense of individual freedoms.

The impact of perception manipulation campaigns cannot be overstated. Public confidence in the judiciary is vital for maintaining its role as a neutral arbiter. Once this confidence is compromised, it becomes challenging to restore. The judiciary must be viewed as impartial to ensure its decisions are respected and upheld. When manipulated narratives cast doubt on this impartiality, the resultant mistrust can have long-term detrimental effects on democratic governance.

Impacts on Free Speech and Press Freedoms

The potential risks posed by Project 2025 to the freedoms of expression and press are significant and multifaceted. One key risk is increased governmental oversight, often presented under the guise of 'fact-checking' or regulation. While fact-checking is crucial in combating misinformation, when controlled by government entities, it can stifle critical journalism. This kind of oversight may easily transition into regulatory frameworks that limit what can be reported, effectively creating a chilling effect that silences dissenting voices.

This chilling effect is not merely theoretical; it undermines the fundamental role of the press in holding power to account. For instance, journalists might refrain from investigating or publishing on sensitive topics due to fear of repercussions, thereby reducing the diversity of viewpoints available to the public. When critical voices are muted or self-censored, society loses the necessary checks and balances that sustain a healthy democracy.

New legislative barriers further compound these issues by imposing onerous requirements on investigative journalism. Such policies disproportionately impact smaller, independent media outlets, which often lack the resources to comply with complex regulations. Consequently, these barriers can sideline vital pieces of journalism that challenge power structures. Independent media has historically played an essential role in uncovering corruption and abuses of power; therefore, hindering their ability to operate freely compromises journalistic freedom.

Another dimension to consider is the possible threats and insufficient protections for whistleblowers. Whistleblowers have been essential in exposing misconduct within governmental and corporate spheres, yet they often face substantial risks. The hostile environment for whistleblowers discourages individuals from coming forward with critical information, leading to less accountability and more unchecked power abuses. Insufficient legal protections mean that those who choose to expose wrongdoing might suffer severe personal and professional consequences, thereby sending a broader message that such actions are unwelcome.

Efforts to control narratives through misinformation campaigns also pose grave risks. When governments engage in or tolerate the spread of misinformation, they exacerbate societal divisions. The manipulation of facts to fit specific agendas creates echo chambers where only reinforcing viewpoints are heard. This erosion of the shared factual basis necessary for public debate undermines diverse viewpoints and hampers constructive dialogue. As a result, the public becomes less informed and more polarized, contributing to an unhealthy democratic environment.

Misinformation campaigns damage the credibility of legitimate sources of information, making it harder for citizens to discern truth from falsehood. This loss of trust in media institutions corrodes the very foundation upon which informed civic participation rests. A populace divided by misinformation is less capable of engaging in reasoned discussion, which is essential for resolving complex social and political issues.

The confluence of these factors—governmental oversight, legislative barriers, threats to whistleblowers, and misinformation efforts—creates a scenario where the freedoms of expression and the press are significantly compromised. Each factor alone is concerning, but together they represent a formidable threat to democratic values.

Increased governmental oversight framed as 'fact-checking' limits the capacity of journalists to critique and investigate those in power without fear of retribution. Legislative barriers make it financially and legally challenging for smaller media outlets to survive and thrive, thus narrowing the field of journalistic endeavors. Threats to whistleblowers further discourage the exposure of wrongdoing, allowing potentially dangerous governmental actions to go unchecked. Finally, misinformation campaigns foment division and impede the free exchange of ideas essential for democracy.

This mosaic of suppression tactics makes it clear that Project 2025 could severely impact the freedoms of expression and press. These freedoms are pillars of democracy, designed to ensure transparency, accountability, and the free flow of information. Without them, the ability of citizens to make informed decisions, hold leaders accountable, and participate meaningfully in democratic processes is drastically diminished.

Possible International Repercussions

When examining the potential global repercussions of Project 2025, it is essential to consider how adverse changes could embolden authoritarian regimes worldwide and shift global views on U.S. democratic principles. Historically, the United States has served as a beacon of democracy. Its actions and policies have inspired movements towards greater freedom and governance reforms in various nations. Any deviation from this path due to Project 2025 might send a signal that authoritarianism is not only tolerated but potentially preferable. This could lead regimes with authoritarian tendencies to feel legitimized in their actions, worsening human rights conditions and curtailing freedoms in their regions.

Moreover, reduced leadership in international human rights as a result of Project 2025 could have dire consequences. The U.S. has long been a vocal advocate for human rights on the global stage. It often uses its influence to pressure other nations into upholding these standards. If Project 2025 results in a more inward-looking U.S., this could weaken the mechanisms that hold violators accountable. Countries where human rights abuses are rampant may see a decrease in external pressures to reform, leading to an increase in violations. This reduction in leadership would also strain relationships with international organizations committed to promoting democracy and human rights. Partnerships that have been built over decades may erode, further diminishing global efforts to uphold these values.

A more isolationist foreign policy approach could hinder international cooperative efforts and reduce support for emerging democracies. Joint initiatives aimed at fostering democracy and development rely heavily on U.S. participation and funding. A shift toward isolationism under Project 2025 would likely result in diminished U.S. involvement in such initiatives. Emerging democracies, which benefit significantly from financial aid, technical assistance, and political backing from established democracies, might find themselves struggling to sustain progress. Furthermore, this could deter other nations from contributing to these efforts, perceiving them as less critical without U.S. leadership.

Allies may recalibrate their foreign policies in response to changes brought about by Project 2025. Nations traditionally aligned with the U.S. based on shared democratic values might seek new alliances if they perceive a waning commitment to these principles. They could adopt more independent or even contradictory stances on key issues, weakening the unified front that has historically stood against authoritarianism and promoted democratic governance. For instance, European allies might enhance their diplomatic ties with other global powers like China or Russia, seeking stability and economic opportunities that the U.S. fails to offer.

Conversely, adversaries could exploit perceived weaknesses for geopolitical leverage. If Project 2025 leads to a perception of U.S. retreat from the global stage, countries like China and Russia may take advantage by expanding their influence. These nations could fill the void left by the U.S. in various regions, promoting their own models of governance. Such shifts would not only alter the balance of power but also challenge the spread of democratic ideals. We could witness increased support for autocratic leaders, aggressive territorial expansions, and a rise in state-sponsored disinformation campaigns aimed at undermining democratic institutions worldwide.

Socio-Political Polarization

Understanding how Project 2025 could exacerbate existing socio-political divides in the United States is crucial in assessing its potential impact on democracy. One key aspect to consider is the implementation of polarizing policies. When policymakers push for initiatives that cater to extreme ideological viewpoints, it can widen the gap between opposing factions. For instance, if Project 2025 introduces measures that strongly favor one political ideology over another, it can deepen existing animosities and make it more challenging for individuals from different backgrounds to find common ground.

Political polarization isn't a new phenomenon in American politics, but it has the potential to escalate significantly through targeted policies. Policies designed to benefit specific interest groups over others can spark resentment among those who feel marginalized or overlooked. This sense of exclusion can foster deeper societal rifts, with affected groups feeling alienated and disenfranchised. For example, if Project 2025 proposes tax cuts for large corporations at the expense of social welfare programs, those who rely on these programs may perceive the government as catering exclusively to the wealthy elite, thereby fueling social and economic divides.

The rise of echo chambers exacerbates this dynamic further. In the age of social media and personalized news feeds, individuals increasingly find themselves within information bubbles that reinforce their existing beliefs while isolating them from countervailing perspectives. These echo chambers reduce opportunities for constructive dialogue by limiting exposure to diverse viewpoints. If Project 2025 includes policies that indirectly encourage such isolation—perhaps by supporting media outlets that cater to niche audiences—it could diminish public discourse's robustness, further entrenching ideological divides.

Historical examples of policy-driven polarization provide valuable context for understanding these dynamics. Consider the aftermath of the Civil Rights Movement in the 1960s. While the legislation aimed to address systemic inequalities, the resistance it faced led to a realignment of political affiliations and heightened regional tensions. Similarly, during the Reagan era, the implementation of conservative economic policies polarized the electorate, leading to intensified political battles over issues like taxation and government spending. Such historical precedents underscore the difficulty of uniting a populace divided by deeply entrenched beliefs—a challenge that Project 2025 might exacerbate.

To better grasp these complexities, it's useful to examine cases where polarizing policies have had tangible effects. For instance, recent immigration policies have illustrated how governmental decisions can amplify divisions. Tougher immigration laws and border enforcement have been celebrated by some sectors while inducing fear and uncertainty among immigrant communities. By prioritizing one group's interests over another's, such policies contribute to a climate of division and mistrust. If Project 2025 adopts similarly divisive stances on contentious issues, it could further strain an already fragile social fabric.

Moreover, the role of leadership cannot be understated. Leaders who champion divisive policies tend to attract support from fervent partisans while alienating moderates and opposition members. This was evident during Donald Trump's presidency when his administration's policies and rhetoric often polarized the nation. The implications for Project 2025 are clear: leadership that favors polarizing initiatives risks deepening societal fissures and making reconciliation efforts increasingly difficult.

In light of these considerations, it becomes evident that Project 2025's approach to policymaking will significantly influence the socio-political landscape. Policymakers must navigate the delicate balance between addressing the needs of various interest groups and maintaining social cohesion. Strategies that prioritize inclusivity and dialogue over partisanship and exclusion should be encouraged to mitigate the risk of exacerbating societal divides.

One practical approach involves fostering bipartisan initiatives. Policies that emerge from cross-party collaboration are more likely to gain broader acceptance and reduce feelings of marginalization. Historically, significant legislative achievements—such as the Social Security Act and the Civil Rights Act—resulted from bipartisan efforts that transcended political divides. Encouraging similar cooperation for Project 2025 could help in tackling contentious issues without exacerbating polarization.

Educational initiatives also play a crucial role in bridging socio-political divides. Programs that promote critical thinking, media literacy, and civic engagement can equip individuals with the skills needed to understand and appreciate differing perspectives. By investing in education, Project 2025 can counteract the rise of echo chambers and foster a more informed and empathetic citizenry.

Additionally, supporting platforms for constructive dialogue is essential. Town halls, community forums, and digital platforms can serve as venues for meaningful conversations between individuals with diverse viewpoints. Facilitating such interactions allows for the exchange of ideas and nurtures mutual understanding. If Project 2025 integrates these principles into its framework, it can create opportunities for healing and reconciliation amid prevailing divisions.

It is equally important to recognize the power of communication in shaping public perception. Transparent and empathetic communication from leaders can bridge gaps and build trust among disparate groups. During times of crisis or conflict, effective communication strategies that emphasize shared values and collective goals can mitigate divisiveness. Ensuring Project 2025 adopts such communication practices will be vital in promoting unity and reducing polarization.

In assessing the potential risks posed to democracy by Project 2025, this chapter has explored several critical dimensions. The proposed measures have substantial implications for civil liberties, including increased surveillance, restrictions on public assembly, and cuts in legal aid. These actions threaten individual freedoms, marginalize vulnerable communities, and undermine democratic principles by fostering an environment of fear and repression. Historical precedents highlight how similar policies have been used to target dissenting voices and weaken social movements advocating for justice and equality.

Moreover, the chapter delves into the far-reaching consequences on judicial independence and free speech. Increased politicization in judge selection, budget cuts, and changes in judicial review standards jeopardize the judiciary's impartiality and effectiveness. Governmental oversight and legislative barriers to press freedom stifle investigative journalism and discourage whistleblowing, while misinformation campaigns erode trust in legitimate sources of information. Together, these factors contribute to socio-political polarization, exacerbate existing divides, and pose significant challenges to maintaining a robust and inclusive democracy.

CHAPTER 4

Your Rights: Identifying Threats

Identifying the threats to your rights is essential for understanding the risks posed by Project 2025. The chapter focuses on the specific rights at risk and offers guidance on recognizing potential threats. By doing so, it aims to equip you with the knowledge needed to safeguard these fundamental freedoms.

This chapter will explore the current legislative actions that threaten the right to assembly and association, detailing how recent laws aim to curtail protests and gatherings. It also examines contemporary threats, such as the use of surveillance technology to monitor activists, which could create an environment of fear and mistrust. Additionally, the chapter provides strategies for community mobilization and legal recourse, highlighting the importance of grassroots organizing and the role of civil rights organizations in defending these rights.

Freedom of Assembly and Association

The rights to assembly and association are cornerstones of a democratic society, allowing individuals to gather, express shared values, and advocate for common goals. These freedoms, enshrined in the First Amendment of the U.S. Constitution, are essential for promoting civic engagement, enabling social movements, and ensuring that diverse opinions have a platform. However, with the advent of Project 2025, these rights face unprecedented threats that jeopardize their very existence.

Overview of Constitutional Guarantees Related to Assembly and Association

Under the First Amendment, the right to peaceful assembly and association is guaranteed. This protection enables citizens to come together for lawful purposes such as protests, political rallies, unions, and community gatherings. The Supreme Court has consistently upheld that these freedoms are fundamental to maintaining a vibrant democracy. For example, in the landmark case *De Jonge v. Oregon* (1937), the Court declared that peaceful assembly for lawful discussion cannot be made a crime. Similarly, in *NAACP v. Alabama* (1958), the Court ruled that compulsory disclosure of NAACP membership lists violated the freedom of association.

These constitutional guarantees provide a vital framework within which citizens can exercise their rights. They ensure that divergent voices can be heard and collective actions can be taken without fear of retribution or censorship by the government. Understanding these legal foundations is critical because they form the backbone of civil liberties and free expression in America.

Recent Legislative Actions Threatening These Rights

Despite these robust protections, recent legislative trends indicate an alarming shift aimed at curtailing assembly and association rights. In response to the rise of social movements and increased public demonstrations, several states have introduced laws designed to suppress protests and gatherings. For instance, states like Florida and Oklahoma have passed "anti-riot" bills that impose severe penalties on protesters and grant immunity to drivers who injure or kill protesters blocking traffic.

These legislative actions represent a significant departure from precedents protecting civil liberties. They reflect a growing tendency to equate peaceful protests with criminal activity, undermining the legitimate exercise of First Amendment rights. The chilling effect of such laws could deter individuals from participating in collective action due to fear of legal repercussions.

In addition to state-level initiatives, there is growing concern about federal measures aimed at limiting assembly rights under the pretext of national security and public order. These developments necessitate vigilance and active resistance to preserve the freedoms of assembly and association.

Analysis of Contemporary Threats, Including Laws Limiting Protests

Contemporary threats to assembly and association rights are multifaceted, involving both direct legislative attacks and broader socio-political dynamics. One of the most pressing issues is the increasing use of surveillance technologies to monitor and intimidate activists. Advanced tools such as facial recognition software and digital tracking are being employed by law enforcement agencies to identify and target protest leaders and participants. This not only infringes on privacy rights but also creates an environment of fear and mistrust.

Moreover, the framing of protests as inherently violent or disruptive events has gained traction in public discourse. Media portrayals often highlight isolated incidents of unrest, painting a distorted picture that fuels support for restrictive measures. This narrative shift makes it easier for authorities to justify harsh crackdowns on assemblies, further eroding democratic freedoms.

Laws explicitly designed to limit protests, such as those restricting the time, place, and manner of demonstrations, pose another significant threat. While regulations on protests must balance public order and safety, overly stringent rules disproportionately impact marginalized communities and stifle dissenting voices. For example, requiring permits for protests can serve as a bureaucratic barrier that delays or prevents spontaneous gatherings, a critical tool for immediate response to social injustices.

Strategies for Community Mobilization and Legal Recourse

Given the growing threats to assembly and association rights, proactive strategies are essential for defending and reclaiming these freedoms. Community mobilization plays a pivotal role in this endeavor. Grassroots organizing, coalition building, and public education campaigns can raise awareness about the importance of assembly rights and push back against restrictive legislation. Engaging with local officials, attending town hall meetings, and leveraging social media platforms can amplify voices and galvanize support for preserving these rights.

Legal recourse is another critical avenue for safeguarding assembly and association freedoms. Civil rights organizations, such as the American Civil Liberties Union (ACLU) and the National Lawyers Guild, offer valuable resources and support for individuals facing legal challenges related to protests. These organizations can provide guidance on navigating the legal system, filing lawsuits, and advocating for policy changes.

Moreover, fostering strong legal defenses for protestors is crucial. Educating citizens about their rights during protests, including understanding permissible actions, documenting encounters with law enforcement, and seeking legal representation when necessary, enhances the resilience of assembly rights. Legal training workshops and know-your-rights seminars empower communities to assert their freedoms confidently.

Voter Suppression Tactics

Voter suppression is a term that encapsulates various legal and illegal actions taken to prevent eligible voters from exercising their right to vote. Historically, this practice has been used to systematically disenfranchise specific groups, particularly minorities and marginalized communities. The origins of voter suppression can be traced back to the post-Reconstruction era in the United States, with tactics such as literacy tests, poll taxes, and grandfather clauses deliberately designed to exclude Black voters. Over the years, these methods evolved, yet the intention remained to undermine the democratic process by hindering equal participation.

In contemporary times, voter suppression manifests through several prevalent tactics, one of the most contentious being voter ID laws. Proponents argue that such laws are necessary to prevent voter fraud, ensuring the integrity of elections. However, numerous studies have shown that instances of voter fraud are exceedingly rare, bringing into question the true motive behind these laws. Voter ID requirements often place undue burdens on certain demographics, including low-income individuals, the elderly, and students, who may lack the resources or documentation necessary to obtain valid identification. By imposing these barriers, voter ID laws effectively reduce voter turnout among these groups, skewing election outcomes.

Another common tactic involves purging voter rolls. This practice entails removing inactive voters from registration lists, ostensibly to maintain up-to-date records. While accuracy in voter rolls is important, the criteria for purging can be overly broad or inadequately communicated, leading to eligible voters being mistakenly removed. When individuals arrive at polling stations only to find they are not on the list, the immediate reaction may be confusion and frustration, resulting in many leaving without casting their ballots.

Gerrymandering, the manipulation of electoral district boundaries to favor a particular party, also plays a significant role in diminishing the voting power of certain groups. Through gerrymandering, political entities can design districts that consolidate or dilute the influence of specific populations, ensuring a predetermined outcome. This erodes the principle of fair representation, allowing elected officials to choose their voters rather than voters choosing their representatives.

Educating voters about their rights and monitoring activities around elections is paramount in combating these suppression tactics. Awareness campaigns, community workshops, and accessible information about voting procedures can empower citizens to overcome obstacles intentionally placed in their path. Knowledge of how to obtain proper identification, understanding the timeline for registering to vote, and knowing what to do if faced with intimidation or misinformation at the polls are critical components of voter education efforts. Additionally, organizations dedicated to observing and documenting election practices play a vital role in holding authorities accountable and advocating for policies that promote inclusivity and fairness.

The broader impact of voter suppression extends beyond individual elections, posing a grave threat to democracy itself. When segments of the population are systematically excluded from the voting process, the government no longer represents the will of all its citizens. This leads to policy decisions and governance that fail to address the needs and interests of the entire populace, fostering disenchantment and distrust in political institutions. Furthermore, the ripple effect of disenfranchisement undermines the legitimacy of electoral outcomes, eroding public confidence in the democratic system.

Addressing the issues of voter suppression requires a multi-faceted approach. Legal challenges to restrictive laws and practices are essential for protecting voting rights. Advocacy groups and concerned citizens must remain vigilant, holding legislators accountable and pushing for reforms that enhance accessibility to the ballot. This includes supporting policies such as automatic voter registration, extended early voting periods, and no-excuse absentee voting, which collectively work to ensure that every eligible voter has the opportunity to participate in elections without unnecessary hindrances.

Community mobilization plays a crucial role in defending voting rights. Grassroots movements and local organizations have historically been at the forefront of fighting voter suppression, mobilizing volunteers to assist with voter registration drives, providing transportation to polling places, and offering legal assistance to those encountering issues at the polls. Collective action strengthens the resilience of communities against efforts to undermine their electoral influence.

Improving monitoring mechanisms is another pivotal aspect in tackling voter suppression. Independent observers and international bodies can provide additional oversight to ensure that elections are conducted fairly and transparently. Transparency in electoral processes fosters trust and encourages greater civic engagement, reinforcing the principles of democracy.

Finally, it is imperative to foster a culture that values and respects the sanctity of the vote. Civic education programs, starting from an early age, can instill an understanding of the importance of voting and the responsibilities that come with it. Emphasizing the role of each citizen in shaping their government helps build a more informed and active electorate, better equipped to resist suppression efforts.

Attacks on Privacy Rights

Privacy rights in the United States have undergone significant changes, particularly with the advent of digital technology and evolving governmental policies. Understanding the legal framework surrounding privacy is pivotal for concerned citizens, especially under Project 2025. This subpoint explores the erosion of privacy rights, identifies present threats, offers tools for safeguarding personal data, and speculates on future regulatory changes.

The legal landscape of privacy rights in the U.S. is complex and multifaceted, rooted primarily in constitutional amendments and federal statutes. The Fourth Amendment of the U.S. Constitution provides protection against unreasonable searches and seizures, thereby establishing a fundamental right to privacy. Additionally, various federal laws like the Electronic Communications Privacy Act (ECPA) and the Privacy Act of 1974 outline specific protections for electronic communications and personal information held by government agencies. Despite these safeguards, loopholes and outdated provisions often fail to address contemporary privacy concerns posed by rapid technological advancements.

One of the most pressing threats to privacy today is government surveillance. Programs like the National Security Agency's (NSA) data collection initiatives have raised alarm among privacy advocates. Under Section 702 of the Foreign Intelligence Surveillance Act (FISA), the NSA can monitor and collect communications between foreign targets and U.S. citizens without a warrant. This mass collection of data, justified under the guise of national security, often leads to incidental surveillance of innocent individuals. Moreover, local law enforcement agencies increasingly use tools like Stingrays—devices that mimic cell towers to intercept mobile phone traffic—and facial recognition software, amplifying concerns about pervasive surveillance.

Another significant threat stems from corporate data collection practices. Companies like Facebook, Google, and Amazon amass vast quantities of personal data through their services. Although users consent to data collection via terms of service agreements, the extent and use of this data often remain opaque. Recent scandals, such as the Cambridge Analytica incident, highlight how personal data can be exploited for purposes beyond user understanding or control. The lack of stringent regulations enables corporations to monetize personal information, further undermining individual privacy.

To safeguard personal data, several tools and strategies can be employed. Firstly, encryption is a vital tool for enhancing digital security. Encrypting emails, messages, and sensitive files ensures that only intended recipients can access the content. Tools such as Signal for messaging and ProtonMail for email provide end-to-end encryption, significantly enhancing communication privacy. Virtual Private Networks (VPNs) are another essential tool, masking users' IP addresses and encrypting internet traffic, thereby protecting online activities from surveillance or tracking.

Additionally, employing strong, unique passwords for different accounts minimizes the risk of data breaches. Password managers like LastPass or 1Password help generate and store complex passwords securely. Enabling two-factor authentication (2FA) adds an extra layer of security, requiring not just a password but also a verification code sent to a mobile device or email.

Users can also reduce data collection by adjusting privacy settings on social media and other online platforms. Limiting the amount of personal information shared publicly and regularly reviewing app permissions can mitigate unnecessary data exposure. Educating oneself about phishing scams and avoiding suspicious links or downloads further enhances online safety.

Speculating on future regulatory changes impacting privacy, we may foresee increased governmental efforts to balance national security with individual privacy rights. Post-2025, there could be heightened scrutiny of surveillance programs and greater demands for transparency and accountability from intelligence agencies. Legislative measures might emerge, seeking to close existing loopholes and ensure stricter oversight of data collection practices.

In the corporate realm, growing public awareness and advocacy for privacy rights could drive new regulations. The introduction of comprehensive federal data protection legislation akin to the European Union's General Data Protection Regulation (GDPR) remains a possibility. Such regulation would enforce stringent requirements on data collection, processing, and storage, granting individuals more control over their personal information.

Furthermore, technological advancements may prompt new challenges and solutions in privacy protection. Developments in artificial intelligence and machine learning could lead to more sophisticated forms of surveillance and data analysis, necessitating innovative countermeasures. Conversely, these technologies might also facilitate improved privacy tools, such as advanced encryption algorithms and decentralized data systems, empowering individuals to safeguard their digital identities more effectively.

In light of these potential shifts, staying informed about privacy rights and advocating for stronger protections is crucial. Collaborating with organizations dedicated to defending civil liberties, such as the Electronic Frontier Foundation (EFF) and the American Civil Liberties Union (ACLU), can amplify efforts to influence policy changes. By actively participating in discussions and supporting legislative initiatives aimed at bolstering privacy protections, citizens can collectively reinforce their rights in an increasingly digital world.

Threats to Minority Protections

Addressing the ongoing risks to protections for minority communities under Project 2025 is a crucial aspect of safeguarding democratic values. Minority communities have historically faced various forms of discrimination, and it is essential to understand existing laws and protections in place to combat these challenges.

To begin with, numerous laws and protections have been established over the years to ensure the rights of minority groups. The Civil Rights Act of 1964 is one of the most significant legislative milestones that prohibited discrimination on the basis of race, color, religion, sex, or national origin. This law laid the foundation for further advancements in securing equality. Additionally, the Voting Rights Act of 1965 was introduced to eliminate racial discrimination in voting, ensuring that minority groups had an equal opportunity to participate in the political process. Over time, other measures such as the Fair Housing Act and the Americans with Disabilities Act have expanded protections, addressing areas like housing discrimination and disability rights.

Despite the existence of these vital laws, recent legislative measures targeting minority groups have raised concerns. For instance, there have been attempts to introduce stricter voter ID laws that disproportionately impact minority voters. These measures often require specific forms of identification that can be difficult for marginalized communities to obtain. Furthermore, some states have enacted laws limiting early voting and same-day registration, which tend to suppress voter turnout among minorities. Another troubling trend is the introduction of bills that restrict access to healthcare for transgender individuals, highlighting an ongoing effort to undermine the rights of certain minority groups.

Given these threats, it is imperative to empower community organizing and advocacy efforts to protect minority rights. Grassroots organizations play a pivotal role in mobilizing communities and advocating for policies that promote equality. For example, groups like the NAACP and the ACLU have long been at the forefront of fighting for civil rights through legal action and public awareness campaigns. Local community groups also contribute significantly by providing resources and support to those affected by discriminatory practices. Encouraging active participation in community organizing helps to amplify voices and fosters a sense of solidarity among minority groups.

Anticipated developments in policy and law will undoubtedly impact minority communities in various ways. It is crucial to stay informed about potential changes that could either strengthen or weaken existing protections. For instance, there may be efforts to expand anti-discrimination laws to cover more aspects of daily life, such as online harassment and hate speech. Conversely, there might be attempts to roll back existing protections under the guise of deregulation or budget cuts. Monitoring legislative developments and court rulings will help communities prepare for and respond to these changes effectively.

Future Outlook on Civil Liberties

The potential trajectory of civil liberties under Project 2025 signals a critical juncture for rights that many have long taken for granted. Concerns about assembly and association, voter suppression, monitoring and privacy, and the role of social movements underscore the urgent need for both awareness and action.

Projections on Assembly and Association Rights Future Trends

As we look toward the future of assembly and association rights under Project 2025, several trends are emerging that could redefine how individuals gather and express collective interests. Legislative changes aimed at limiting protests can already be seen in recent years, with measures such as increased penalties for unauthorized gatherings and restrictions on public spaces used for demonstrations.

These legislative actions raise profound questions about the balance between maintaining public order and protecting democratic freedoms. There is a genuine concern that these trends will continue to erode the ability of citizens to organize and speak out against injustices. If unchecked, these measures could set precedents that limit not just physical assembly but also digital forms of association, where new regulations might govern online group interactions and gatherings.

It's crucial to monitor these legislative developments closely and advocate for laws that protect rather than inhibit the right to assemble. Engaging with policymakers, participating in public forums, and leveraging legal channels to challenge unconstitutional restrictions can help safeguard these essential freedoms.

Examination of the Evolving Landscape of Voter Suppression

Voter suppression has long been a tool for disenfranchising specific demographics, and its evolving landscape under Project 2025 is no exception. Various states have introduced more stringent voter ID laws, which disproportionately affect minority communities, the elderly, and economically disadvantaged groups who may find it difficult to obtain the necessary identification.

Additionally, changes to polling locations and hours present significant challenges. Reduced access to convenient and accessible voting centers forces many voters to travel further and wait longer, effectively discouraging participation. This tactic particularly impacts disabled individuals and those without flexible work schedules, further widening the gap in voter turnout.

The suppression doesn't stop there. Challenges to voter registration processes, such as purges of voter rolls and increased scrutiny of registration applications, present additional barriers. These measures often result in eligible voters being turned away at the polls or finding their registrations invalidated without notice.

To counteract these efforts, grassroots responses have proved effective. Community-led initiatives that educate voters on their rights, assist with acquiring proper identification, and provide transportation to polling stations are vital. Legal challenges against discriminatory practices and lobbying for more voter-friendly legislation can also help reverse this troubling trend.

Impact of New Technologies on Monitoring and Privacy Rights

New technologies have revolutionized many aspects of life, but they also pose significant risks to monitoring and privacy rights. Surveillance tools like facial recognition software and data analytics have become increasingly sophisticated, enabling both government and private entities to track individuals more precisely than ever before.

This heightened level of surveillance raises concerns about privacy invasions and the potential misuse of personal information. Governments may argue that these technologies enhance security and public safety; however, without robust oversight and regulation, the risk of abuse is considerable. Unwarranted surveillance can lead to chilling effects where individuals feel constrained in their expressions and associations due to fear of being monitored.

The rapid development of these technologies necessitates updated privacy laws that reflect contemporary challenges. Advocating for transparency in how data is collected, stored, and used, as well as pushing for stronger encryption standards to protect personal information, are essential steps toward preserving privacy rights.

For individuals, adopting tools like encrypted communication apps and becoming educated on privacy best practices can offer some level of protection. Moreover, supporting organizations that fight for digital rights and holding tech companies accountable for ethical data use is paramount in this ongoing battle.

Role of Social Movements in Shaping Future Protections

Social movements play a pivotal role in shaping future protections for civil liberties. Historically, movements like the Civil Rights Movement and LGBTQ+ rights advocacy have driven substantial legislative changes and societal shifts. In the context of Project 2025, social movements are likely to continue as primary catalysts for defending and expanding rights.

Mobilizing communities to demand change requires strategic planning and sustained effort. Modern social movements often utilize digital platforms to reach broader audiences, coordinate actions, and amplify messages. This digital activism can be powerful, but it also makes movements vulnerable to cyber-attacks and digital surveillance, emphasizing the need for secure communication channels.

Movements must also focus on building coalitions across different sectors and demographics. By uniting varied interest groups, they can create stronger and more resilient networks capable of enacting meaningful change. Educational campaigns that inform the public about rights and current threats, combined with direct actions like protests and lobbying, contribute to a multi-faceted approach that increases the pressure on policymakers.

Legal support is another critical aspect of social movements. Ensuring that individuals and organizations involved in activism have access to legal advice and representation helps protect them from retaliatory actions and strengthens their capacity to challenge unjust laws and policies.

In this chapter, we have explored the critical importance of the freedoms of assembly and association within a democratic society. These rights, fundamental to civic engagement and public discourse, face significant threats under Project 2025. We have analyzed how recent legislative actions at both state and federal levels aim to curtail these freedoms, often under the pretense of maintaining public order or national security. These developments not only undermine the legal framework that safeguards our right to peaceful assembly but also contribute to an environment where dissenting voices may be suppressed through intimidation and punitive measures.

To counter these emerging threats, proactive strategies are essential. Community mobilization, grassroots organizing, and public education about these rights can help build resilient defenses against restrictive legislation. Legal recourse, supported by civil rights organizations, offers another avenue to protect and reclaim these freedoms. By staying informed and engaged, citizens can advocate for policies that uphold the democratic principles enshrined in the Constitution. Preserving the rights to assembly and association requires concerted effort and vigilance to ensure that diverse opinions continue to find a platform and collective actions can occur without fear of retribution.

CHAPTER 5

Empowerment Through Knowledge

Empowerment through knowledge is essential for any society aiming to preserve and advance its democratic values. In this chapter, we explore the profound impact of understanding political and legal frameworks on individual empowerment. This understanding enables citizens to navigate their rights effectively and engage meaningfully in democratic processes. With a clear grasp of these concepts, individuals are better equipped to protect their liberties and contribute to the functioning of a just society. The exploration of these themes underscores the importance of civic education as a tool for fostering engaged and informed communities.

The chapter delves into several key areas critical for empowering citizens through knowledge. The foundational principles of the United States Constitution, including the separation of powers, checks and balances, and federalism, are thoroughly examined for their roles in maintaining democratic governance. Additionally, the chapter sheds light on the Bill of Rights and the protections it affords individual freedoms, emphasizing how these principles prevent governmental overreach. Readers will gain insights into the functioning of both federal and state governments, understanding their respective roles and responsibilities. Finally, the chapter addresses the significance of civic organizations and educational programs in promoting awareness and engagement, thereby equipping citizens with the tools necessary to advocate for their rights and hold leaders accountable.

Basic Principles of the U.S. Constitution

The American Constitution serves as the bedrock of democracy and individual rights, structuring the way the government operates and protects its citizens. One of its key principles is the separation of powers, a concept ensuring that no single branch of government can dominate the others. The Constitution divides power among the legislative, executive, and judicial branches to maintain checks and balances. The legislative branch, represented by Congress, creates laws. The executive branch, led by the President, enforces these laws. Meanwhile, the judicial branch, headed by the Supreme Court, interprets the laws and ensures they align with the Constitution.

This separation of powers promotes accountability and prevents the concentration of power, which could lead to authoritarian rule. By having each branch operate independently while being able to limit the actions of the others, the system protects the democratic process. For instance, the President can veto legislation, but Congress can override this veto with a two-thirds majority. Similarly, the judiciary can declare laws unconstitutional, checking the powers of both Congress and the President. This interplay ensures that all branches work within their constitutional limits.

Another fundamental component of the Constitution is the Bill of Rights. These first ten amendments guarantee essential personal freedoms and protect citizens from governmental overreach. Among these rights are freedoms of speech, religion, and assembly, as well as the right to a fair trial and protection against unreasonable searches and seizures. These amendments emerged from the Founding Fathers' desire to ensure that individual liberties would remain safeguarded in the new nation. The First Amendment, for example, allows individuals to express their opinions freely without fear of government retaliation. This amendment forms the cornerstone of free society and vibrant public discourse.

Moreover, the Fourth Amendment's protection against unreasonable searches and seizures ensures that citizens have a right to privacy. Law enforcement agencies must obtain warrants based on probable cause before conducting searches, thereby preventing arbitrary intrusions. Such protections underscore the importance of personal freedoms in maintaining a just and democratic society.

Federalism is another integral principle enshrined in the Constitution. It refers to the division of power between the federal government and state governments, allowing different levels of governance to address various issues more effectively. The federal government handles matters of national importance, such as defense, foreign policy, and interstate commerce. In contrast, state governments manage local concerns, including education, transportation, and public safety.

This dual system of governance helps tailor policies to the specific needs of communities while maintaining national cohesion. For example, states can enact laws that reflect their unique cultural and economic conditions, fostering innovation and responsiveness. At the same time, the federal government can coordinate efforts across states to address overarching challenges, ensuring consistency and unity in critical areas.

Checks and balances are crucial mechanisms designed to prevent any branch of government from becoming too powerful. These measures allow each branch to monitor and restrict the actions of the others, maintaining equilibrium. Congress can pass legislation, but the President can veto it. However, Congress can override this veto with a supermajority vote. The judiciary can review laws and executive actions, declaring them unconstitutional if they violate the principles of the Constitution. Additionally, Congress holds the power to impeach and remove the President or other federal officials for misconduct, ensuring accountability at the highest levels of government.

Understanding the principles of checks and balances is essential for concerned citizens and activists alike. By recognizing how each branch can limit the power of the others, individuals can better advocate for transparency and the rule of law. For instance, during times of political turmoil, knowing that the judiciary can act as a check on potential executive overreach reassures citizens that democratic norms will be upheld. Furthermore, activists can leverage these mechanisms to hold leaders accountable, using legal avenues to challenge unjust policies or actions.

In summary, the Constitution's principles of the separation of powers, the Bill of Rights, federalism, and checks and balances form the foundation of American democracy and individual rights. The separation of powers ensures independent operation among the government's branches, promoting accountability and preventing tyranny. The Bill of Rights guarantees essential personal freedoms and protects citizens from governmental overreach. Federalism allows for a division of power between federal and state governments, enabling tailored responses to local needs while maintaining national coherence. Checks and balances provide mechanisms for each branch to limit the actions of the others, preserving the balance of power and upholding democratic principles.

Functioning of Federal and State Governments

Understanding the roles and responsibilities of federal and state governments is critical for citizens to engage effectively with both levels of government. The federal government focuses on overarching national issues such as defense, immigration, and currency regulation. These are areas that require a unified approach to ensure the country's security and stability.

For example, the Department of Defense (DoD) manages military policies and operations necessary to protect the nation from external threats. By understanding how the DoD operates and its priorities, citizens can better appreciate the complexities of national security. Similarly, agencies like U.S. Citizenship and Immigration Services (USCIS) oversee the legal parameters of immigration, impacting people across the country. Currency regulation, managed by entities such as the Federal Reserve, affects the economy, influencing inflation rates and financial policies that touch every citizen's life.

In contrast, state governments are more focused on local issues that directly impact residents' daily lives. Responsibilities include managing education systems, building and maintaining infrastructure, and overseeing local law enforcement.

For example, state departments of education make decisions about curriculum standards, teacher certifications, and funding allocations for schools. This means that the quality of education varies significantly from state to state, giving residents a direct reason to engage with their local officials. Infrastructure projects like road construction and public transportation are also managed at the state level. State governments allocate resources to ensure these projects serve community needs efficiently.

Local law enforcement agencies, under state jurisdiction, maintain public safety, manage emergency responses, and enforce state laws. Understanding who to contact for various issues can help citizens address concerns effectively, whether reporting a crime or participating in community policing initiatives.

The interrelation between federal and state governments adds another layer of complexity. They collaborate on various issues while occasionally finding themselves in conflicts due to differing priorities or interpretations of laws.

One prime example of collaboration is disaster response. Federal agencies like FEMA work with state and local governments to provide relief and recovery efforts. During events like hurricanes or wildfires, federal support is crucial for comprehensive aid, but local knowledge ensures that help arrives where it's most needed. Conflicts often arise over environmental regulations. States may have stricter laws than federal guidelines, leading to disputes. For instance, California has historically implemented more stringent automobile emissions standards than those set by the federal government, resulting in legal battles.

Citizens must understand these dynamics to navigate government agencies effectively. Engaging with bureaucracy can seem daunting, but knowing the correct pathways and procedures empowers individuals to advocate for change.

First, identify the appropriate agency for your concern. Federal issues might involve contacting your congressional representative or specific federal departments. State issues usually require reaching out to local representatives or state agencies. Creating a clear, concise message is vital when addressing government officials. Whether writing a letter or making a phone call, clearly state your issue, why it matters, and what action you desire.

Additionally, attending town hall meetings or public forums offers an opportunity to engage with officials directly. These events provide a platform to voice concerns, ask questions, and gain insights into how government decisions are made. Many government agencies also have online portals where citizens can submit inquiries or track the progress of ongoing issues. Utilize these digital tools to stay informed and connected with the actions being taken on your behalf.

Finally, understanding the appeals process is essential. If a decision does not go in your favor, knowing how to appeal can ensure your voice is heard. Each agency typically outlines its appeals process online or provides this information upon request.

Role of Civic Organizations and Institutions

Civic organizations play a pivotal role in enhancing democracy and empowering citizens. These organizations include any group formed to promote the public good, often through volunteer efforts or community involvement. Examples of civic organizations range from local neighborhood associations to large international non-profit entities. They work towards various objectives such as social justice, environmental conservation, and human rights advocacy. By fostering civic engagement, these groups help people understand their political and legal rights and encourage active participation in democratic processes.

Nonprofit organizations significantly impact voter education and rights protection. They often provide resources and programs aimed at informing citizens about their voting rights, registration processes, and the importance of participating in elections. For instance, organizations like the League of Women Voters and Rock the Vote conduct extensive outreach campaigns to engage underrepresented communities. They educate voters on candidates' platforms and issues at stake, enabling informed decision-making at the polls. Additionally, nonprofits work tirelessly to protect voter rights, fight against disenfranchisement, and ensure that elections are free, fair, and accessible to all eligible citizens.

The contributions of these nonprofits extend beyond electoral processes. Many also offer essential community services, addressing needs ranging from housing and healthcare to education and employment. These services empower individuals by providing them with the tools and support necessary for personal and community development. For example, Habitat for Humanity builds affordable housing for low-income families, while local food banks ensure that communities have access to nutritious meals. Such initiatives demonstrate the broad scope of nonprofit work and its direct impact on enhancing the quality of life for many individuals.

Grassroots movements are equally important as they drive political change from the bottom up. These movements often start at the community level, where individuals come together to address specific local issues. Over time, they can grow to influence national policies and societal norms. The civil rights movement in the United States, for example, began with small, localized efforts to challenge racial segregation and discrimination. Through persistent advocacy, organized protests, and strategic litigation, it ultimately led to significant legislative and social changes, including the Civil Rights Act and the Voting Rights Act.

Grassroots activism fosters community involvement and strengthens democracy by giving a voice to ordinary citizens. It emphasizes the power of collective action and the importance of engaging with others to achieve common goals. Movements like Black Lives Matter and the environmental activist group Extinction Rebellion illustrate how grassroots efforts continue to shape public discourse and policy. These movements harness social media and other modern communication tools to mobilize support, spread awareness, and compel authorities to address pressing issues related to social justice and environmental sustainability.

Educational institutions also play a crucial role in promoting civic awareness and engagement. Schools and universities are not only places of academic learning but also environments where young people develop an understanding of their civic duties and rights. Curriculums that include civics education ensure that students are well-versed in the workings of their country's political and legal systems. Programs focused on mock elections, debates, and student councils provide practical experience in democratic participation.

Higher education institutions often serve as hubs for political activism and discourse. Universities host lectures, seminars, and workshops that delve into critical social and political issues, encouraging students to think critically and engage in meaningful discussions. Student-led organizations on campus advocate for various causes, from LGBTQ+ rights to climate change policies. By fostering such an environment, educational institutions prepare the next generation of leaders who are informed, engaged, and ready to contribute positively to society.

Moreover, partnerships between educational institutions and civic organizations can amplify their impact. Collaborative efforts might include service-learning opportunities where students apply classroom knowledge to real-world scenarios, working on community projects or volunteering with local nonprofits. Such experiences not only benefit the community but also enhance students' understanding and commitment to civic responsibilities.

Navigating Legal Rights and Resources Available

Understanding our legal rights forms the bedrock of our engagement in democratic processes. To empower citizens effectively, it is crucial to have a thorough understanding of the essential rights guaranteed under both federal and state law. Knowing these rights not only ensures we can protect ourselves when necessary but also enables us to advocate for others within our community.

Federal laws provide a broad spectrum of rights that apply nationwide. These include fundamental rights such as freedom of speech, freedom of assembly, and the right to due process. Additionally, the Bill of Rights enshrines other critical protections like the right to a fair trial, protection against unreasonable searches and seizures, and guarantees against cruel and unusual punishment. State laws further add another layer, often providing more specific or additional protections tailored to local circumstances. For instance, some states offer stronger privacy protections or more comprehensive anti-discrimination laws than those at the federal level.

With a solid understanding of these rights, individuals are better positioned to navigate the complexities of legal systems. However, simply knowing one's rights is often insufficient without access to the necessary tools and resources that enable effective utilization of these rights. This is where utilizing legal resources becomes vital.

There are various resources available to assist citizens in accessing their rights. Legal aid organizations provide free or low-cost legal services to individuals who may not be able to afford private attorneys. These organizations often specialize in areas such as housing, immigration, employment, and family law, offering invaluable support to those in need. Furthermore, many non-profit organizations focus on educating citizens about their rights through workshops, informational pamphlets, and online resources. Websites like LegalZoom and Nolo also provide accessible information on a wide range of legal topics, helping individuals better understand their legal standing and options.

For those interested in deeper engagement, participating in legal advocacy offers a powerful avenue for effecting change. This can involve a variety of activities, from lobbying for new legislation to filing lawsuits that challenge unjust laws or practices. Litigation, in particular, has been a cornerstone of civil rights movements throughout history. Landmark cases such as Brown v. Board of Education and Roe v. Wade demonstrate the profound impact litigation can have in advancing societal progress.

Individuals can participate in legal advocacy both directly and indirectly. Direct participation might include working with advocacy organizations to draft policy proposals or taking part in public demonstrations to raise awareness. Indirectly, one can support these efforts by donating to legal funds, volunteering time and expertise, or amplifying the voices of those directly involved in the struggle for justice. Advocacy is not limited to high-profile cases; everyday efforts to address local issues can lead to significant change over time.

Community legal education programs play an essential role in this empowerment process. These programs aim to inform and educate communities about their legal rights and how to exercise them. Often run by non-profits, universities, and local government entities, they provide training sessions, workshops, and seminars on various legal topics. This grassroots approach to legal education helps demystify the law, making it more accessible and less intimidating to ordinary citizens.

Educational initiatives often focus on practical aspects, such as understanding tenant rights, navigating the criminal justice system, or recognizing employment discrimination. By bringing legal knowledge to the community level, these programs foster a more informed citizenry capable of advocating for themselves and others. Schools, libraries, and community centers frequently serve as hubs for these educational activities, ensuring they reach a broad audience.

Moreover, collaboration between legal professionals and community organizations enhances the effectiveness of these programs. Lawyers, paralegals, and law students often volunteer their time to lead workshops or provide pro bono services. This partnership ensures that the information disseminated is accurate, up-to-date, and relevant to the specific needs of the community.

To maximize the impact of legal education, it is important for these programs to be inclusive and culturally sensitive. Communities are diverse, and legal issues can vary widely depending on cultural, economic, and social contexts. Tailoring educational content to address these differences ensures that all community members, regardless of their background, can benefit from these initiatives.

Checks and Balances in Practice

Checks and balances play a crucial role in maintaining the integrity of democratic systems by ensuring that no single branch of government gains unchecked power. Real-world applications of this system underscore its importance and effectiveness. Take, for instance, the case of Watergate in the 1970s. The U.S. Congress and the judiciary played pivotal roles in uncovering the Nixon administration's misconduct. Congressional committees conducted investigations and held hearings, while the Supreme Court ruled that the president could not use executive privilege to withhold crucial evidence. This demonstrates how checks and balances can function effectively to expose wrongdoing and hold high-ranking officials accountable, ultimately leading to President Nixon's resignation.

Another example is the restriction on President Truman's attempt to take control of steel mills during the Korean War. In Youngstown Sheet & Tube Co. v. Sawyer, the Supreme Court ruled that the president did not have the authority to seize private property without Congressional approval, highlighting an effective judicial check on executive power. Such instances show that the checks and balances system is not merely theoretical but has practical, impactful outcomes.

Citizen involvement is another critical aspect of maintaining the checks and balances system. Citizens need to be vigilant and knowledgeable about potential breaches of this system. For instance, public awareness and activism were instrumental in the recent exposure of abuses in various governmental programs. Media outlets and whistleblowers often bring these issues to light, but it is public pressure and activism that usually drive change. Citizens can recognize breaches by staying informed through reliable news sources, participating in town hall meetings, and engaging with advocacy groups that monitor governmental actions.

One practical way for citizens to act upon breaches is by contacting their representatives, organizing or joining advocacy groups, and leveraging social media platforms to raise awareness. It's also important for citizens to vote in both local and national elections to ensure that accountable individuals are placed in positions of power. Participatory vigilance ensures that the checks and balances system remains functional and robust.

Accountability mechanisms within the legislative, executive, and judicial branches are designed to impose checks on each other. Legislators, for example, can conduct oversight hearings, subpoena documents, and impeach officials who engage in illegal activities. The executive branch, via veto power and executive orders, can limit legislative overreach. Meanwhile, the judicial branch has the authority to review and nullify laws and executive actions that violate the Constitution.

Consider the process of impeachment as a significant accountability mechanism. The U.S. Congress holds the power to impeach the president and other high-ranking officials, demonstrating a direct check by the legislature on the executive branch. Similarly, the confirmation process of federal judges serves as a check by the legislative branch on the judiciary, ensuring that appointed judges adhere to constitutional principles.

Efforts to maintain balance among the branches require constant vigilance, adaptability, and proactive measures. Legislative bodies must continually refine regulations and policies to adapt to new challenges while preserving fundamental democratic principles. For example, after significant financial crises or scandals, new laws and regulations often emerge to prevent recurrence. This continuous adaptation is essential to addressing emerging threats and vulnerabilities.

Moreover, balance maintenance involves collaboration between branches. Each branch must respect the boundaries of the others while remaining assertive in exercising its own powers. A collaborative yet assertive approach helps ensure that no one branch undermines the functioning of the others. Educational programs and public awareness campaigns also play critical roles in maintaining this balance. These initiatives can help citizens understand the importance of checks and balances, and encourage engagement in democratic processes.

Furthermore, transparency and open communication between branches can mitigate potential conflicts and foster cooperation. This includes regular briefings, reports, and public disclosures that keep all branches informed and aligned with constitutional norms. Public institutions, such as schools and universities, should also incorporate education on checks and balances into their curricula to build a more informed citizenry.

Understanding political and legal frameworks is an essential aspect of empowering citizens. This chapter has explored the U.S. Constitution's fundamental principles, including the separation of powers, the Bill of Rights, federalism, and checks and balances. Each of these elements plays a crucial role in maintaining democracy and protecting individual rights. By comprehending these mechanisms, citizens can better safeguard their freedoms and engage more effectively in democratic processes.

The chapter also highlighted how federal and state governments operate, emphasizing the importance of knowing who to contact for specific issues. Additionally, it addressed the role of civic organizations in enhancing democracy through education and advocacy. Recognizing and navigating one's legal rights further empowers individuals to participate actively in societal reforms. Overall, this knowledge equips concerned citizens, activists, educators, and political professionals with the tools necessary to promote transparency, accountability, and democratic values.

CHAPTER 6

Practical EngagementStrategies

Effective political engagement requires practical strategies that empower citizens to actively participate in the democratic process. This chapter delves into the foundational aspects of civic involvement, focusing on how individuals can navigate and influence their political landscape. By providing a comprehensive guide on voter registration, various voting methods, researching candidates and ballot measures, and promoting community initiatives, readers will gain the tools necessary to make informed decisions and enhance their impact within their communities.

The chapter begins by outlining the steps required to register to vote, emphasizing the importance of understanding state-specific regulations and deadlines. It then explores the different methods of voting, such as early voting, absentee voting, and traditional in-person voting, helping readers identify which option suits their circumstances best. Additionally, the significance of informed voting is highlighted through guidance on researching candidates and ballot measures using nonpartisan resources. Finally, the chapter underscores the power of community engagement by discussing ways to encourage voter participation at the local level, including organizing registration drives and educational workshops. Through these actionable steps, readers will be equipped to foster robust civic involvement and contribute meaningfully to the democratic process.

Registering to vote and participating in elections

Voting is a fundamental aspect of civic engagement and serves as the cornerstone of a functioning democracy. It empowers citizens to make decisions about their government and influence policies that affect their daily lives. Understanding the steps involved in the voter registration process, the various methods available for voting, researching candidates and ballot measures, and encouraging participation through community initiatives are essential for ensuring robust civic involvement.

To begin with, the voter registration process is a critical first step in becoming an active participant in the electoral process. It is important to be aware of the specific deadlines and requirements for registration in your state, as they can vary considerably. For instance, some states allow online registration, while others may require paper forms. Additionally, the deadlines for registration might differ depending on whether you're registering for a primary or general election. Many states provide comprehensive resources on their official websites, making it easy to find the necessary information and complete the registration process. Taking advantage of these online resources can streamline the process and ensure that you meet all the requirements well before the deadline.

Once registered, understanding the different methods of voting available can enhance your participation. Early voting is an option that allows voters to cast their ballots ahead of Election Day, providing flexibility for those who may have scheduling conflicts. Absentee voting, another method, enables individuals who cannot physically visit polling stations to vote by mail. This is particularly beneficial for military personnel, students studying out of state, or anyone with mobility issues. In-person voting remains the traditional method, where voters go to designated polling stations on Election Day. Each of these methods has its advantages, and it's crucial to choose the one that best fits your circumstances to ensure your voice is heard.

Informed voting is equally important, and this requires diligent research into candidates and ballot measures. Using nonpartisan resources can help you obtain unbiased information that allows you to make educated decisions. Websites like Ballotpedia or VoteSmart provide detailed profiles on candidates, including their political stances, voting records, and endorsements. Similarly, organizations such as the League of Women Voters offer comprehensive guides on ballot measures, explaining their potential impacts and the arguments for and against them. Engaging with these resources ensures that your vote is based on a thorough understanding of what each candidate and measure represents.

Beyond individual efforts, encouraging voter participation within your community can amplify the impact of your engagement. Community initiatives play a vital role in mobilizing voters, especially those who might feel disenfranchised or uninformed. Organizing voter registration drives at local events or workplaces can help ensure that everyone has the opportunity to register. Hosting informational sessions or workshops on the voting process and the importance of civic participation can educate and empower community members. Additionally, facilitating conversations about upcoming elections and key issues among friends and family can foster a culture of engagement and collective responsibility.

Voter registration is more than just a procedural task; it's a gateway to significant civic involvement. By staying informed about deadlines and utilizing available resources, you can navigate the registration process with ease. Once registered, taking the time to explore different voting methods ensures that you can participate in a way that aligns with your lifestyle and commitments. Whether opting for early voting, absentee voting, or in-person voting, each method offers a way to make your voice heard.

Engaging in thorough research about candidates and ballot measures is essential for casting an informed vote reflecting your values and priorities. Utilizing nonpartisan resources helps cut through the noise of partisan rhetoric, allowing for a clearer understanding of each option on the ballot. This level of preparation not only empowers you as a voter but also contributes to the overall health of the democratic process by fostering well-informed electorates.

Encouraging voter participation extends beyond personal actions and taps into the power of community. Community-based efforts to promote voting can create a ripple effect, reaching those who might otherwise feel excluded from the electoral process. Organizing registration drives, educational workshops, and discussions about the importance of voting can demystify the process and inspire broader participation. These initiatives are particularly effective in underrepresented communities, where systemic barriers often deter potential voters.

Joining civic groups and community organizations

Identifying local civic organizations and community groups can be a pivotal step in fostering collective action and support. These groups often serve as the backbone of local activism, offering individuals an opportunity to unite around common goals and values. To begin, it is essential to conduct thorough research on the various civic organizations operating within your locality. This involves exploring their mission statements, reviewing past activities, and understanding their core values to ensure alignment with your personal beliefs.

For instance, if environmental conservation is a priority for you, look for organizations dedicated to sustainability efforts or ecological preservation. Similarly, those passionate about social justice may seek out groups focused on advocacy for racial equality or human rights. By aligning yourself with organizations that reflect your values, you become part of a collective voice striving towards shared objectives. This alignment not only enhances personal satisfaction but also reinforces the organization's mission through increased membership and active engagement.

Amplifying one's voice through organized efforts is another significant advantage of joining civic organizations. When individuals come together under a unified cause, they gain strength in numbers. Collective action enables members to pool resources, share knowledge, and exert greater influence than any single person could achieve alone. For example, coordinated campaigns such as letter-writing drives, public demonstrations, or social media initiatives can draw attention to critical issues and compel policymakers to respond.

Engaging in community organizations also fosters a sense of solidarity and resilience among members. The collaborative environment encourages open dialogue, where diverse perspectives are shared, and innovative solutions can be developed. Through these interactions, individuals gain a deeper understanding of the complexities surrounding various issues, enhancing their capacity to advocate effectively. Additionally, the support systems within these groups provide encouragement and motivation, reducing feelings of isolation and fostering a sense of belonging.

Active participation is crucial for maximizing the benefits of civic organization membership. Volunteering your time and skills to these groups can have a profound impact. Whether it's participating in organized events, attending regular meetings, or contributing specific expertise, every effort counts towards achieving the group's goals. Volunteering not only aids the organization but also offers personal growth opportunities, allowing you to develop new skills, expand your network, and build lasting relationships.

Moreover, becoming actively involved allows you to stay informed about ongoing initiatives and upcoming events. Regular attendance at meetings provides insight into the strategic planning process, enabling you to contribute ideas and feedback directly. It also offers a platform for you to express your concerns and aspirations, ensuring that your voice is heard within the group. Sharing your unique skills, whether it's in areas like communications, logistics, or fundraising, can significantly enhance the effectiveness of the organization's operations.

Conducting needs assessments is another vital component of effective civic engagement. Understanding the specific challenges and priorities of your community allows civic organizations to tailor their actions accordingly. Needs assessments involve gathering data through surveys, interviews, or public forums to identify pressing issues and potential solutions. This evidence-based approach ensures that the group's efforts are targeted and impactful, addressing real problems rather than perceived ones.

For example, a community might face issues related to inadequate public transportation. By conducting a needs assessment, a civic organization can gather data on residents' transportation habits, preferences, and barriers. This information can then be used to advocate for improved services, propose new routes, or initiate carpool programs, directly responding to the community's needs. Effective needs assessments also promote inclusivity by engaging diverse voices, ensuring that marginalized groups are represented in decision-making processes.

Successful execution of needs assessments requires a systematic approach. Begin by defining the scope and objectives of the assessment, clarifying the questions you aim to answer. Next, choose appropriate methods for data collection, considering factors like accessibility and representativeness. Analyzing the collected data involves identifying trends, gaps, and potential areas for intervention. Finally, communicate the findings to stakeholders, including community members and policymakers, to drive informed action.

Lobbying and direct advocacy techniques

Practical Engagement Strategies

Lobbying serves as a crucial mechanism through which individuals and groups can represent their interests and concerns to policymakers. At its core, lobbying involves the organized effort of influencing decision-makers within legislative bodies to enact favorable policies or oppose unfavorable ones. Whether advocating for environmental protections, healthcare reforms, or educational improvements, lobbying ensures that diverse viewpoints are considered in the policymaking process. This advocacy plays an integral role in shaping policies that align with public needs and preferences.

Building relationships with policymakers is fundamental to effective lobbying. Establishing a rapport with elected officials and their staff requires consistent and respectful communication. Different methods can be employed to foster these relationships, including face-to-face meetings, phone calls, emails, and social media interactions. Each method has its unique advantages. For instance, personalized meetings allow for more direct and impactful discussions, whereas social media can help maintain regular contact and public visibility. It's important to approach these communications with professionalism, clarity, and knowledge about the issues at hand. Regular, meaningful interactions help build trust and make it more likely that policymakers will consider your perspectives seriously.

Crafting clear and impactful advocacy messages is another essential aspect of lobbying. Effective communication hinges on presenting well-researched data combined with compelling personal stories. Data provides the empirical evidence needed to substantiate claims, while personal anecdotes humanize the issue, making it more relatable to policymakers. By weaving together statistical information and emotional narratives, advocates can deliver powerful messages that resonate both logically and emotionally. Preparing detailed fact sheets, infographics, and testimonials in advance can aid in presenting a strong case during meetings or correspondence with legislators.

Organizing campaigns and events is a strategic way to mobilize community involvement and garner broader support for advocacy efforts. Community-driven events such as town hall meetings, rallies, and informational workshops serve dual purposes: they raise awareness about specific issues and demonstrate a collective demand for policy action. Effective campaign organization requires meticulous planning and coordination, from setting clear objectives and timelines to engaging volunteers and utilizing media channels for promotion. Engaging local media can amplify the reach and impact of these events, attracting more participants and gaining the attention of policymakers.

To summarize, successful lobbying and direct advocacy to influence policymakers involve several practical steps. Understanding the definition and role of lobbying is the first step, recognizing it as an organized effort to represent various interests in the legislative process. Building strong relationships with policymakers through varied communication methods helps establish trust and ensures ongoing dialogue. Crafting advocacy messages that blend solid data with personal stories creates compelling arguments that capture both the logical and emotional aspects of the issues. Lastly, organizing community campaigns and events effectively mobilizes public support and demonstrates to policymakers the broad base of backing for specific policy changes. These strategies, when implemented thoughtfully and consistently, can significantly enhance one's ability to engage meaningfully in the political process and drive substantive change.

Engaging with local and national representatives

Engaging with elected officials and influencing decision-making at various government levels is a crucial aspect of active citizenship. To effectively impact the political landscape, it is essential to understand who your representatives are and what they stand for. This involves researching local, state, and federal representatives, understanding their positions on key issues, and knowing their voting records.

Begin by identifying your representatives at each level of government. Websites such as Vote Smart or official government portals can provide comprehensive information about elected officials based on your address. It is useful to keep track of their office contact details, which will facilitate direct communication later.

After identifying your representatives, delve into their policy positions and legislative history. Understanding where they stand on important issues helps you tailor your communication and advocacy efforts. Reading their speeches, campaign material, and news articles can offer insights into their priorities and values. Additionally, reviewing their voting records on platforms like GovTrack can help you understand their stance on specific policies, which is particularly important when advocating for or against certain legislation.

Direct communication is one of the most effective strategies for engaging with elected officials. Preparing for meetings and writing impactful emails are two key methods of direct communication. When preparing for a meeting, take the time to thoroughly research the issues you plan to discuss. Outline your main points clearly and succinctly, ensuring that you highlight how these issues impact you and your community. Personal anecdotes can be powerful tools in illustrating your points and making your case more compelling.

When writing emails, clarity and brevity are crucial. Begin with a concise subject line that indicates the purpose of your email. In the body of the email, clearly state the issue you are addressing, why it is important, and what action you would like the representative to take. Be respectful and courteous, even if you disagree with the representative's stance. Providing factual information and personal stories can strengthen your message.

Participating in organized lobby days and advocacy events is another effective way to engage with elected officials. These events are often coordinated by advocacy groups or non-profit organizations and provide structured opportunities to meet with policymakers. Lobby days typically involve training sessions to equip participants with the knowledge and skills needed to advocate effectively. They may also include scheduled meetings with representatives or their staff members, during which participants can present their concerns and discuss potential solutions.

Advocacy events, such as rallies or town halls, offer additional platforms for citizens to voice their opinions and raise awareness about critical issues. These events can amplify individual voices by bringing together like-minded individuals and creating a collective impact. By participating in these events, you demonstrate your commitment to the cause and contribute to a broader movement for change.

Follow-up techniques are essential for maintaining ongoing dialogue and building lasting relationships with elected officials. After a meeting or event, sending a thank-you note is a courteous way to express appreciation for the representative's time and attention. In the note, briefly reiterate the key points discussed and any commitments made during the meeting. This reinforces the importance of the issue and keeps it on the representative's radar.

Additionally, periodic follow-ups can help keep the conversation going and demonstrate continued interest in the matter. Regularly update the representative on developments related to the issue and any new information that may be relevant. This ongoing engagement not only strengthens your relationship with the representative but also ensures that the issue remains a priority.

Building a network of supporters can also enhance your advocacy efforts. Connecting with other concerned citizens, advocacy groups, and community organizations can amplify your voice and create a more substantial impact. Collaboration allows for sharing resources, strategies, and information, making your collective efforts more effective.

By leveraging social media, you can further engage with your representatives and mobilize others. Platforms like Twitter and Facebook enable direct communication with elected officials and allow you to share your message with a broader audience. Engaging in online discussions, sharing relevant articles, and using hashtags can help raise awareness and build support for your cause.

Staying informed and mobilizing others

Encouraging continuous education on political issues and fostering community-wide participation is essential for maintaining a healthy democracy. To begin with, educating oneself on current candidates, ballot measures, and policy issues is crucial. Staying informed about who is running for office and what they stand for allows citizens to make well-informed decisions at the polls. Candidates often present differing views on various issues, including healthcare, education, the economy, and more. By thoroughly researching their platforms, voters can align their choices with personal values and the needs of their communities. Additionally, understanding ballot measures—proposals decided by public vote—enables citizens to directly influence laws and policies that impact their daily lives.

To ensure the information gathered is accurate and unbiased, it is essential to seek out nonpartisan resources. Nonpartisan organizations and websites provide valuable, impartial summaries and analyses of candidates, measures, and policy issues without promoting a specific agenda. Utilizing these resources helps cut through the noise of partisan politics, allowing voters to base their decisions on facts rather than rhetoric. Examples of reputable nonpartisan resources include organizations like the League of Women Voters, Ballotpedia, and the Center for Responsive Politics. These platforms offer comprehensive guides and comparisons that break down complex issues into understandable terms.

Furthermore, attending local debates, town halls, and forums provides firsthand insights and enhances political engagement. These events offer unique opportunities to hear directly from candidates and policymakers about their visions and plans. Engaging in such settings allows citizens to ask questions, express concerns, and gauge the authenticity and competence of those seeking office. For instance, town halls are particularly beneficial as they foster direct interaction between elected officials and their constituents, promoting transparency and accountability. Regular participation in these events ensures that the voices of ordinary citizens are heard and considered in the political process.

Mobilizing friends, family, and community members to participate in the democratic process is another vital aspect of fostering engagement. Encouraging others to stay informed and get involved creates a ripple effect that amplifies collective influence. This could involve organizing voter registration drives, hosting informational meetings, or simply discussing political issues over casual gatherings. Sharing reliable information and resources within one's network helps build a politically aware and active community. By uniting individuals with common interests and goals, grassroots movements can be sparked, leading to significant social and political changes.

For a more structured approach, identifying local organizations focused on civic engagement can provide further support and resources. Local advocacy groups and community organizations often play a pivotal role in driving political participation. They offer educational programs, facilitate discussions, and organize events designed to raise awareness and inspire action. Involvement in these groups not only enhances individual knowledge but also strengthens collective efforts to address community-specific issues. Platforms such as local government websites and community boards can be instrumental in discovering these groups and their initiatives. By actively participating in or supporting local organizations, citizens can contribute to broader efforts that extend beyond individual actions.

It is also beneficial to understand the diversity of civic groups available, from local advocacy organizations to national movements. These groups address a wide range of issues, including environmental advocacy, social justice, economic reforms, and more. Joining forces with like-minded individuals within these groups can amplify one's voice and impact. The collaborative nature of civic organizations enables them to organize more effectively, pool resources, and implement strategies that might be challenging for individuals working alone. Showcasing this diversity and the various issues these groups tackle can help citizens find organizations that resonate with their values and interests.

While fostering community-wide participation is vital, creating accessible platforms for learning and engagement is equally important. Online resources, social media, and local libraries can serve as effective tools for disseminating information and facilitating discussions. Hosting workshops, webinars, and interactive sessions can also enhance understanding and encourage active involvement. Ensuring that these resources are easily accessible to all community members promotes inclusivity and equal opportunity for participation. This approach not only educates but also empowers individuals to take meaningful actions.

Incorporating practical steps and guidelines within these educational efforts can significantly enhance their effectiveness. For example, conducting needs assessments can help identify the most pressing issues within a community and tailor educational programs accordingly. By addressing specific concerns and providing relevant information, these programs become more impactful and engaging. Furthermore, training sessions on how to evaluate sources of information for bias and reliability can equip citizens with the skills needed to navigate the often overwhelming influx of data during election cycles.

This chapter has outlined various actionable steps for citizens to effectively engage in the political process, emphasizing the importance of voter registration, informed voting, and community participation. By understanding the procedures for registering to vote and the different voting methods available, individuals can ensure their voice is heard in elections. Additionally, conducting thorough research on candidates and ballot measures allows voters to cast informed ballots that reflect their values. Beyond personal actions, encouraging others to participate through community initiatives can further strengthen democratic engagement and create a more robust political environment.

Incorporating these practices into daily life not only empowers individual citizens but also fosters a sense of collective responsibility within communities. Staying informed about political issues and mobilizing others to engage actively can lead to significant social and political changes. By supporting local civic organizations and participating in grassroots movements, citizens can amplify their impact and address community-specific concerns more effectively. These efforts contribute to a more informed electorate and healthier democracy, ensuring that diverse viewpoints are represented and respected in the political process.

CHAPTER 7

Organizing Your Community

Organizing your community for collective action is instrumental in creating significant social and political change. Community organization can transform isolated voices into a powerful chorus, enabling citizens to address shared concerns and wield influence effectively. Understanding the methods and principles behind organizing a community is crucial for anyone looking to initiate or amplify grassroots movements. This chapter provides an examination of these essential strategies, offering readers both theoretical frameworks and practical advice on mobilizing community efforts for sustained impact.

In this chapter, you will explore various techniques for starting a grassroots movement, including how to identify local issues and recruit dedicated volunteers. We delve into the importance of crafting clear visions and mission statements to guide collective efforts. The role of effective communication is thoroughly examined, outlining how to tailor messages to different audiences for maximum engagement. Additionally, we discuss the significance of utilizing local resources, from influential leaders to community spaces, ensuring that every possible advantage is leveraged. Finally, the chapter offers insights into forming coalitions and alliances, underscoring the power of collaboration in achieving long-term goals. Through detailed analysis and actionable steps, this chapter aims to equip readers with the tools needed to organize their communities successfully.

Building a Grassroots Movement

Initiating a Grassroots Movement

Starting a successful grassroots movement requires careful planning and adherence to several core principles. By understanding the community's needs, attracting dedicated volunteers, articulating a clear vision, and utilizing local resources, we can effectively mobilize community members for advocacy.

Identifying Local Issues

The first fundamental principle in initiating a grassroots movement is identifying local issues. Engaging with the community to gather insights on pressing concerns is essential. Begin by conducting surveys or holding small focus group discussions to understand the community's most urgent issues. This could involve door-to-door canvassing, setting up booths at local events, or using digital tools like online questionnaires. The goal is to capture a broad spectrum of opinions from various demographics within the community. Listening attentively to people's concerns will not only highlight critical issues but also build trust and a sense of ownership among community members.

Once you have gathered enough data, analyze the findings to pinpoint recurring themes and patterns. Highlighting these common concerns helps to establish a collective understanding of what the community faces. Remember, the effectiveness of a grassroots movement often hinges on its ability to address issues that significantly impact the daily lives of citizens. Therefore, ensuring that the concerns are genuinely reflective of the community's experience is crucial.

Recruiting Volunteers

After identifying the local issues, the next step is recruiting volunteers who are passionate about addressing these problems. Utilizing social media platforms can be highly effective in spreading awareness and attracting potential volunteers. Create engaging posts that clearly state the movement's purpose and call for volunteers. Use visuals, videos, and personal stories to make the content more relatable and shareable. Hosting live sessions or webinars can provide a platform for direct interaction, allowing potential volunteers to ask questions and understand how they can contribute.

In addition to social media, organizing or participating in community events can help attract volunteers. Events such as town hall meetings, local fairs, or neighborhood cleanups provide opportunities to meet people face-to-face and discuss the movement. Distributing flyers and pamphlets at these events with information about how to get involved can further boost volunteer recruitment. It's important to create an inclusive environment where everyone feels their input and effort will be valued, which fosters motivation and participation.

Creating a Clear Vision and Mission Statement

With a growing pool of volunteers, it becomes imperative to create a clear vision and mission statement that resonates with the community's needs and desires. A well-articulated vision provides a long-term direction for the movement, while a mission statement outlines the specific actions needed to achieve the vision. These statements should reflect the concerns identified during the initial engagement phase and offer a pathway toward solutions.

Writing a compelling vision and mission statement involves several steps. First, revisit the core issues your community highlighted and think about the ultimate changes you hope to see. For example, if affordable housing is a key concern, your vision might be, "A community where everyone has access to safe and affordable housing." The mission statement would then detail how you plan to realize this vision, such as through advocacy for policy changes or developing community-led housing projects.

Make sure to involve your volunteers and other stakeholders in drafting these statements. Their input ensures that the vision and mission resonate across different segments of the community and instill a sense of shared purpose. Once finalized, publicize your vision and mission widely through newsletters, social media, and at community gatherings to keep everyone aligned and motivated.

Utilizing Local Resources

Building momentum for your grassroots movement also requires tapping into local resources. Community leaders often hold significant influence and can lend credibility to your cause. Reach out to respected individuals in the community, including religious leaders, local politicians, and heads of community organizations. Their endorsement can attract more support and open doors to additional resources.

Another valuable resource is community spaces, such as libraries, schools, and parks, which can serve as venues for meetings, workshops, and events. Holding activities in familiar and accessible locations makes it easier for community members to participate and stay engaged. Partnering with local businesses can also yield benefits, such as sponsorships or donations of goods and services. Many businesses are willing to support causes that improve the community, as it enhances their reputation and customer loyalty.

Consider creating committees or workgroups focused on different aspects of the movement, such as fundraising, outreach, or event planning. This allows for better organization and efficient use of available resources. Each committee should have clear objectives and be empowered to make decisions within their scope, fostering a collaborative environment where ideas can flourish.

Engagement and Sustained Effort

While the initial stages of starting a grassroots movement are critical, maintaining engagement and sustaining effort over time are equally important. Regularly updating the community on progress, celebrating small victories, and continuously seeking feedback ensure ongoing participation and adaptability. Providing training and development opportunities for volunteers keeps them motivated and equipped to handle emerging challenges.

Effective Communication and Messaging

Strategic communication plays a pivotal role in organizing communities for collective action and influence. To mobilize and educate community members effectively about the movement's objectives, it's crucial to communicate strategically and thoughtfully. This involves a series of steps that ensure the message not only reaches the intended audience but also resonates with them deeply.

One of the first steps in strategic communication is identifying the target audience. Analyzing demographic data can provide valuable insights into the makeup of the community. This analysis should include age, gender, socioeconomic status, education levels, and other relevant factors that can help segment the audience based on their interests and concerns. For example, younger audiences might be more receptive to messages delivered through social media platforms, while older demographics may prefer traditional channels such as newsletters or in-person meetings. Understanding these preferences allows organizers to tailor their communication strategies more effectively.

Once the target audience is identified, the next step is crafting clear and compelling messages. Complex ideas should be simplified into straightforward terms to ensure they are easily understood by everyone. One effective way to do this is by using analogies or metaphors that relate to everyday experiences. Additionally, incorporating visuals such as infographics, diagrams, and videos can help break down intricate concepts and make the information more accessible. For instance, a grassroots movement focused on environmental conservation could use before-and-after images to illustrate the impact of pollution and the benefits of conservation efforts.

Choosing the right communication channels is another critical aspect. In today's digital age, traditional platforms like newspapers and flyers coexist with digital media including social media, email newsletters, and websites. Each platform has its unique strengths and can reach different segments of the community effectively. Social media, for example, offers a fast and interactive way to engage with the audience, share updates, and create viral content that can reach a broader audience quickly. Meanwhile, newsletters and community bulletin boards can provide detailed information and regular updates to those who may not be as active online. Combining these methods ensures comprehensive coverage and reinforces the message across multiple touchpoints.

Another essential element is encouraging two-way communication. This means creating opportunities for community members to ask questions, share their opinions, and provide feedback. Organizing Q&A sessions can address common queries and misconceptions, fostering greater understanding and support for the movement's goals. Workshops and interactive events provide hands-on experiences that can deepen engagement and commitment. Feedback mechanisms, such as surveys and suggestion boxes, allow community members to voice their concerns and contribute ideas, ensuring that the movement remains responsive to their needs and perspectives.

In addition to these primary steps, several guidelines can enhance the effectiveness of strategic communication. First, maintain consistency in messaging across all channels and interactions. Consistent messages reinforce the core objectives and values of the movement, building trust and credibility among community members. Second, leverage storytelling techniques to create an emotional connection with the audience. Personal stories and testimonials from community members can humanize the movement and make it more relatable. Third, regularly evaluate and adjust communication strategies based on feedback and changing circumstances. This adaptability ensures that the movement remains relevant and continues to resonate with the community over time.

Let's delve deeper into each guideline. Consistency in messaging is crucial because it prevents confusion and misinterpretation. When the same message is delivered uniformly across all channels, it becomes easier for community members to understand and remember the key points. This can be achieved by developing a communication plan that outlines the core messages and the appropriate language and tone for different platforms.

Storytelling, on the other hand, taps into the human ability to connect with narratives emotionally. Stories have the power to inspire, motivate and move people to action. By sharing real-life examples and personal experiences, the movement can create a sense of urgency and importance around its objectives. For instance, a story about a local resident overcoming challenges through community support can highlight the tangible benefits of collective action.

Lastly, evaluating and adjusting communication strategies is an ongoing process that keeps the movement dynamic and effective. Regular assessments can identify what's working well and what needs improvement. For example, if a particular social media campaign gains significant traction, it indicates a strong resonance with the audience, which can inform future strategies. Conversely, if certain messages aren't getting the expected response, it might be necessary to rethink the approach or explore alternative channels.

Hosting Events and Rallies

Organizing public events and rallies is a cornerstone strategy for mobilizing community support and raising awareness. These gatherings serve as focal points where concerned citizens can converge, share their concerns, and collectively amplify their voices. The successful organization of such events necessitates meticulous planning and logistics, effective engagement with influential speakers and performers, strategic marketing, and rigorous measurement of success and impact.

To begin with, the foundation of any successful event lies in comprehensive planning and logistics. It is essential to set clear objectives that define what the event aims to achieve. Whether it is to raise awareness about a specific issue, garner support for a cause, or mobilize the community for collective action, clear goals provide direction and purpose. Once the objectives are established, creating a detailed timeline becomes the next critical step. This timeline should outline all necessary tasks from the inception of the idea to the conclusion of the event. Key milestones might include securing permits, booking venues, organizing transportation, and arranging for amenities such as seating, sound systems, and refreshments. By breaking down these tasks into manageable chunks and assigning them specific deadlines, organizers can ensure that no aspect of the event is overlooked.

The engagement of speakers and performers plays a vital role in drawing interest and participation. Selecting individuals who are influential and resonate with the community can significantly enhance the impact of the event. These could be local leaders, activists, artists, or experts whose insights and performances align with the event's objectives. Their participation not only attracts attendees but also adds credibility and depth to the discussions and activities planned. To effectively engage speakers and performers, early outreach is crucial. Providing them with a clear understanding of the event's goals, themes, and logistics ensures they can prepare appropriately and contribute meaningfully. Including diverse voices and perspectives can further enrich the event, making it more inclusive and representative of the community's concerns and aspirations.

Marketing the event is another critical component that determines its reach and effectiveness. In today's digital age, social media campaigns offer a powerful tool for promoting public events and rallies. Platforms such as Facebook, Twitter, Instagram, and LinkedIn allow organizers to create event pages, share updates, and connect with potential attendees. Utilizing hashtags, engaging visuals, and compelling storytelling can help spread the word and build anticipation. Collaborating with local organizations amplifies this effort by tapping into established networks and communities. Partnering with schools, businesses, non-profits, and other community groups broadens the event's visibility and appeal. Traditional marketing methods such as flyers, posters, and press releases should not be neglected, especially for reaching audiences that might not be active on social media.

Measuring the success and impact of an event is crucial for understanding its effectiveness and informing future efforts. Gathering participant feedback provides invaluable insights into what worked well and what could be improved. This can be achieved through surveys, interviews, or suggestion boxes during or after the event. Questions should cover various aspects, including the venue, speaker quality, relevancy of content, and overall experience. Quantifying engagement metrics, such as attendance numbers, social media interactions, and media coverage, offers concrete data to assess the event's reach and impact. Analyzing this data helps determine whether the event met its objectives and how it influenced the community's awareness and support for the cause.

Understanding that each event serves as a building block towards larger goals, organizers must continuously refine their strategies based on feedback and results. For instance, if participant feedback indicates logistical issues, future events could allocate more resources to venue management or transportation coordination. Similarly, analyzing engagement metrics might reveal which promotional strategies were most effective, allowing organizers to focus their efforts where they yield the highest returns.

Incorporating real-life examples can provide valuable insights and inspiration for those organizing public events and rallies. For instance, consider the Women's March held in Washington, D.C., and around the world in 2017. This event exemplified meticulous planning, influential speaker engagement, robust marketing, and post-event impact assessment. Organizers set clear objectives to advocate for women's rights and made extensive use of social media to galvanize participants globally. The inclusion of high-profile speakers and performers drew significant attention, while widespread media coverage amplified the event's message. Post-march analyses highlighted its profound impact on subsequent activism, illustrating the power of well-organized public events in driving social change.

Another example is the climate strikes inspired by Greta Thunberg. These events leveraged the influence of a young activist to mobilize millions worldwide, emphasizing the importance of engaging resonant figures. Social media played a pivotal role in marketing these events, demonstrating how digital platforms can unite global communities around shared causes. Feedback and engagement metrics from these strikes showed a surge in environmental awareness and advocacy, underscoring the effectiveness of strategic event planning.

Finally, it is important to recognize the ripple effects of successful public events and rallies. These gatherings often serve as catalysts for sustained activism, inspiring participants to remain engaged and continue advocating for their cause. They also build momentum for future initiatives, creating a sense of unity and collective purpose within the community. By fostering connections among participants, events and rallies lay the groundwork for ongoing collaboration and coalition-building, essential components of long-term grassroots movements.

Forming Coalitions and Alliances

In any community organization effort, the power of collaboration through the formation of coalitions and alliances cannot be overstated. Coalitions bring together diverse groups to work toward common goals, thereby amplifying their collective impact. This subpoint delves into the crucial aspects of building these alliances, from identifying potential allies to creating a resilient support network, ensuring effective and sustainable community action.

To begin with, identifying potential allies is a critical first step in forming a successful coalition. This involves assessing the mission and work of prospective partners to ensure alignment in vision and objectives. For instance, if your goal is to advocate for environmental sustainability, potential allies might include local environmental NGOs, community gardening clubs, or educational institutions with sustainability programs. Conducting thorough research and holding preliminary discussions can help ascertain whether their long-term goals and methods are compatible with your movement. Understanding each group's strengths and areas of expertise will also pave the way for more fruitful collaborations.

Once potential allies are identified, the next vital step is to create a partnership framework that outlines shared goals and roles. Such a framework provides clarity and helps avoid misunderstandings that could hamper progress. A well-defined framework should detail the specific contributions expected from each partner, be it funding, manpower, or expertise. For example, one organization might take charge of public awareness campaigns, while another handles event logistics. Clear communication during the initial stages of partnership formation ensures that all parties are on the same page and committed to the coalition's success.

Leveraging resources and expertise by pooling knowledge, manpower, and funds is another key aspect of effective coalition building. Each participating group brings unique strengths to the table, and tapping into this collective reservoir can significantly boost the movement's capacity. For example, a coalition working on housing rights might benefit from the legal expertise of advocacy groups, the organizational skills of community leaders, and the funding capabilities of philanthropic organizations. By sharing resources, each group can maximize its impact without overextending its resources. Moreover, joint efforts in fundraising can lead to more significant financial support than individual attempts, enabling more extensive and impactful projects.

Another important consideration when forming coalitions is building resilience within the movement. Social and political landscapes are often dynamic, requiring adaptability to maintain momentum and achieve long-term success. Cultivating a solid support network involves regular communication and meetings to revisit and revise strategies as needed. Flexibility in approach allows the coalition to respond effectively to new challenges and opportunities. For instance, a sudden policy change might necessitate a shift in focus or tactics, and having a robust network ensures the coalition can pivot swiftly and cohesively. Additionally, fostering strong relationships among allied groups creates a sense of solidarity, which is essential for weathering periods of adversity.

Furthermore, celebrating small wins and recognizing each member's contributions can bolster morale and reinforce the commitment to the coalition's larger goals. Public acknowledgment of these achievements, through social media shout-outs or community events, not only motivates existing members but also attracts new supporters.

In conclusion, the importance of collaboration through forming coalitions and alliances in community organizing cannot be overstated. Identifying potential allies who share your mission and values sets the foundation for a strong partnership. Creating a clear framework outlining shared goals and roles ensures all parties have a mutual understanding, leading to more efficient and effective collective action. Leveraging the combined resources and expertise of coalition members amplifies the impact of your efforts and opens up more avenues for positive change. Finally, building resilience through adaptability and cultivating a supportive network enables the coalition to endure and thrive despite inevitable challenges. By adhering to these principles, community organizers can enhance their ability to enact meaningful and lasting change.

Utilizing Local Resources

To build a movement and sustain advocacy, leveraging community assets is crucial. The first step in this process is identifying local leaders and influencers who can amplify the message and rally support. Local leaders often have established trust within the community and can act as gatekeepers to broader networks. Influencers, whether they are formal or informal, possess the charisma and connectivity needed to disseminate the movement's goals effectively. By partnering with these key figures, you gain not only their endorsement but also access to their followers, which can exponentially increase the reach of your message.

Next, establishing partnerships with local businesses and organizations for logistical and financial support is vital. These entities often have the resources that grassroots movements lack, such as venues for events, supplies, and monetary contributions. Businesses and organizations benefit from these collaborations as well, gaining positive public relations and demonstrating corporate social responsibility. It's important to approach these potential partners with clear proposals outlining mutual benefits. For instance, a local coffee shop might provide refreshments for meetings in exchange for recognition on promotional materials. Such partnerships strengthen the movement by providing essential resources while fostering a sense of community solidarity.

Accessing community spaces for meetings, events, and other activities is another key element in organizing a successful community movement. Public libraries, schools, parks, and community centers are often underutilized resources that can serve as excellent venues for gatherings. These spaces are familiar and accessible to residents, making it easier for individuals to participate. When choosing a location, consider factors like accessibility, capacity, and available amenities. For example, hosting a town hall meeting at a local school gymnasium can draw a larger crowd due to its central location and ample parking. Utilizing these communal spaces helps to create an inclusive environment where everyone feels welcome and involved.

Using storytelling techniques to illustrate the urgency and importance of the cause locally is an effective way to engage and motivate community members. Stories resonate deeply because they humanize the issue, making abstract concepts more relatable. Sharing personal anecdotes, case studies, or historical examples can evoke empathy and drive action. To craft a compelling narrative, focus on highlighting individual experiences that reflect the broader challenges the community faces. For instance, telling the story of a family affected by housing insecurity can highlight the need for affordable housing initiatives. Integrating these stories into speeches, social media posts, and marketing materials can help to foster a stronger emotional connection with the audience.

Furthermore, developing a framework for continuous support and engagement is crucial. This means setting up regular check-ins with local leaders and influencers to keep them updated and involved. It also involves maintaining open lines of communication with business partners and organizations to ensure ongoing support. Scheduling regular community meetings or forums allows for continuous dialogue and feedback, helping to adjust strategies and respond to new challenges. Establishing a digital presence through newsletters, social media updates, and online forums ensures that the movement remains visible and active, further solidifying its presence in the community.

In addition to leveraging these community assets, it is important to educate and empower community members. Providing training sessions on advocacy, public speaking, and organizing can equip individuals with the skills needed to take on leadership roles within the movement.

Workshops and seminars can be organized in collaboration with experts and activists, ensuring that participants receive high-quality instruction. Empowered community members are more likely to stay engaged and contribute actively, thereby sustaining the movement over time.

Another aspect to consider is recognizing and celebrating achievements, both big and small. Publicly acknowledging milestones and contributions can boost morale and demonstrate progress. Whether it's a social media shout-out or an appreciation event, recognizing the efforts of individuals and groups keeps spirits high and fosters a sense of accomplishment. These celebrations also serve as reminders of the collective power and progress made, motivating continued involvement and support.

Lastly, evaluating the effectiveness of these strategies is essential for sustained advocacy. Regular assessments help to understand what's working and what needs improvement. Surveys, feedback forms, and participatory evaluations can provide valuable insights from community members. Analyzing this data enables fine-tuning of tactics and strategies, ensuring that the movement remains dynamic and responsive to the community's needs. Continuous improvement based on feedback reinforces the movement's legitimacy and demonstrates a commitment to inclusivity and effectiveness.

The chapter has explored various methods to organize communities for collective action and influence. It highlighted the importance of understanding local issues, recruiting dedicated volunteers, and creating a clear vision and mission. By emphasizing effective communication strategies, such as crafting relatable messages and choosing appropriate channels, the chapter demonstrated how grassroots movements can mobilize community members. Additionally, it underscored the significance of utilizing local resources, forming coalitions, and hosting events to sustain advocacy efforts.

Moving forward, the key to building a successful grassroots movement lies in continuous engagement and adaptability. Regular updates, celebrating victories, and seeking community feedback ensure sustained involvement and responsiveness to emerging challenges. By leveraging community assets, such as local leaders and spaces, movements can strengthen their foundation and broaden their impact. Ultimately, the principles outlined in this chapter serve as a comprehensive guide for fostering community-driven change, empowering citizens, activists, and political professionals to effectively advocate for democratic values and social reform.

CHAPTER 8

Navigating Misinformation

Navigating misinformation is essential for maintaining informed civic engagement and upholding democratic values. In the digital age, the rapid dissemination of information on social media platforms and news sites means that false narratives can quickly gain traction. Recognizing the strategies employed in spreading misinformation allows individuals to develop a critical mindset toward the content they encounter daily. This chapter explores methods for discerning reliable from unreliable information, providing readers with tools to better navigate the digital information landscape.

The chapter delves into the definitions of misinformation and disinformation, highlighting their distinct characteristics. It addresses how emotionally charged language and sensationalized headlines manipulate readers' emotions to spread misleading content. Furthermore, it explains the importance of identifying credible sources through transparent authorship and substantive evidence. The role of algorithms in shaping information and creating echo chambers is examined, alongside strategies for diversifying one's media consumption. Additionally, the chapter discusses the economic incentives driving misinformation, the impact of deepfakes, and the crucial roles of educational institutions and professional organizations in promoting media literacy. Through these explorations, readers will be equipped with practical guidelines to identify and counteract misinformation effectively, fostering a more informed and resilient democratic society.

Recognizing misinformation and disinformation

In today's fast-paced digital age, distinguishing between accurate information and misleading content is crucial for informed civic engagement. Knowing the definitions of misinformation and disinformation is the first step toward this goal. Misinformation refers to inaccurate information that is spread without harmful intent. Examples include outdated statistics or misinterpreted facts shared in good faith, often without malicious purposes. On the other hand, disinformation denotes deliberately misleading information aimed at political erosion or causing harm. For instance, fabricated stories or manipulated media intentionally designed to deceive readers fall under this category. Understanding these definitions helps us navigate through the vast amounts of information encountered daily.

A common tactic employed in spreading misinformation involves the use of emotionally charged language. Headlines laden with sensationalized terms like "shocking" or "unbelievable" can distort facts and evoke strong emotional reactions, prompting readers to share the content without verifying its accuracy. This manipulation of emotions is a strategy used to increase engagement—likes, shares, and comments—regardless of the information's veracity. Furthermore, articles featuring sensationalized headlines often mask the lack of substantial evidence within the body of the text. By recognizing such tactics, readers can maintain a critical stance, questioning the reliability of the information presented.

Another significant aspect to consider is the identification of unreliable sources. There are several indicators to help in assessing the credibility of an information source. Firstly, the lack of credible authorship or transparency serves as a red flag. Reliable articles typically have clear bylines and offer information about the authors' credentials and affiliations, lending credibility to their work. In contrast, dubious websites might either omit author information or provide vague details. Secondly, sensational claims lacking substantive evidence should be treated with caution. When a piece of news makes extraordinary claims but fails to provide verifiable data or references from reputable sources, it warrants skepticism. A guideline here would be to check if the information can be verified by multiple independent and credible sources. If it can't, it's likely not trustworthy.

Additionally, it's essential to understand the role of algorithms in shaping the information we receive. Social media platforms and search engines employ personalized algorithms designed to tailor content based on individual user preferences. While this creates a convenient and engaging online experience, it also has the unintended consequence of creating echo chambers. In these echo chambers, users are predominantly exposed to information that aligns with their existing beliefs and opinions, reinforcing biases and limiting exposure to diverse perspectives. To counter this, it's important to actively seek out varied viewpoints by following a range of news sources and engaging in discussions with people holding different perspectives. An effective guideline is to periodically review and adjust social media settings to ensure a broader spectrum of information is received.

Consider the case of a viral social media post claiming that a particular public figure made controversial statements. Without verification from multiple reliable news outlets, sharing such information contributes to the spread of potential misinformation. Instead, checking the original source of the statement, looking for video evidence, or confirming through established news organizations can prevent the dissemination of falsehoods.

Moreover, understanding the economic incentives behind misinformation can illuminate why certain content spreads rapidly. Websites generating revenue through advertisements may prioritize clicks over content accuracy, producing clickbait headlines aimed at attracting as much traffic as possible. These sites benefit financially from high engagement rates, regardless of the reliability or quality of the information they share. By being aware of these motives, readers can better evaluate the integrity of the sources they encounter.

Educational institutions and professional organizations play pivotal roles in promoting media literacy and critical thinking skills. Incorporating media literacy programs into school curriculums ensures that future generations are equipped to handle the complexities of the information landscape. Such programs teach students how to identify credible sources, verify facts, and recognize biases, empowering them to make informed decisions. Similarly, professional workshops and continuous learning opportunities for adults can reinforce these skills, keeping them updated on evolving tactics of misinformation and disinformation.

The advent of deepfakes—synthetic media where a person's likeness is superimposed onto another's—presents another layer of complexity. Deepfake technology can create highly convincing yet entirely fabricated videos that can mislead viewers regarding events or statements purportedly made by public figures. To combat this, several technology companies and research organizations are developing tools to detect and label deepfake content. Staying informed about such advancements can help individuals remain vigilant against increasingly sophisticated forms of misinformation.

Critical media literacy skills

Evaluating sources is a foundational skill for assessing media accuracy. Not all news outlets uphold the same editorial standards, and understanding these differences can help readers discern credible information from potentially misleading content. One technique is to look at the reputation of the news outlet itself. Established organizations like The New York Times, BBC, or The Washington Post have long-standing editorial guidelines and a history of accountability, making them generally reliable. Conversely, newer sites without a track record or transparency about their funding may be less trustworthy.

Another important aspect of evaluating sources is examining the authors or contributors. Credible articles often come from journalists with recognized expertise in their fields or a consistent history of ethical reporting. Readers can check the author's background, previous work, and affiliated organizations to gauge credibility further. Additionally, peer-reviewed journals and publications with rigorous editorial processes tend to offer more reliable content, especially on technical and scientific topics.

Assessing the editorial standards of news outlets also involves understanding their ethical guidelines. For example, reputable outlets adhere to standards such as presenting balanced viewpoints, fact-checking before publishing, and issuing corrections for mistakes. Readers should seek out these policies often listed on the publication's website, to determine the outlet's commitment to accurate and ethical journalism.

Analyzing content structure can uncover many layers of potential misinformation. Headlines are particularly critical because they shape first impressions and often dictate whether someone will click on an article. Readers should critically assess if headlines accurately represent the article's content or if they are sensationalized to attract clicks. Clickbait tactics, which use exaggerated or emotional language to lure readers, can indicate lower-quality journalism or misleading content.

The role of images in media cannot be overstated. Images can evoke strong emotional responses and can sometimes mislead if taken out of context. Readers should consider whether the images directly relate to the article content and whether they are used responsibly. Reverse image searches can verify the originality and context of visual content. This practice helps expose instances where images are reused or manipulated to support false narratives.

Clickbait headlines and emotionally charged images often appear together, making it crucial for readers to dissect both critically. Recognizing such tactics can help individuals avoid falling prey to misleading or sensationalist journalism. It is also essential to note that some outlets employ these methods not necessarily to deceive but to drive traffic and revenue, which can still compromise the integrity of the information presented.

Fact-checking practices form another pillar of media literacy. Established fact-checking sites like Snopes, FactCheck.org, and PolitiFact serve as invaluable resources. These platforms rigorously verify claims made in various forms of media and provide readers with evidence-based conclusions. Cross-referencing information across multiple trusted sources is another effective strategy. If several reputable outlets report the same facts, the information is likely accurate.

Additionally, reverse image searches can debunk visual misinformation. With tools like Google Images, readers can trace a photograph's origins and usage history. This method reveals whether an image has been previously published and under what circumstances, helping to identify any potential manipulation or misrepresentation. Even social media posts and viral images should undergo this scrutiny, as they are common vectors for misinformation.

Questioning narratives encourages a deeper level of skepticism and inquiry. Readers should routinely ask, "Who benefits?" from the dissemination of specific information. This question can uncover underlying biases or agendas that might not be immediately apparent. For example, during election cycles, certain narratives may be promoted to sway public opinion in favor of particular candidates or policies.

Challenging assumptions also involves recognizing one's biases. Confirmation bias, where individuals favor information that confirms their preexisting beliefs, can cloud judgment. By actively seeking out diverse perspectives and questioning their own viewpoints, readers can develop a more balanced understanding of complex issues.

Moreover, understanding the financial and political affiliations of media outlets can provide insights into potential biases. For instance, knowing that a news organization receives funding from particular interest groups can shed light on why certain topics are covered in specific ways. Transparency about sponsorships and partnerships often helps readers discern any external influences affecting content.

Encouraging skepticism does not mean dismissing all information as false but rather promoting a habit of thoughtful engagement. Critical thinking skills enable readers to analyze the motives behind stories and recognize when information serves particular interests rather than the public good. This practice fosters a discerning audience capable of navigating the complexities of modern media landscapes.

Reliable sources for accurate information

In the modern digital landscape, distinguishing reliable sources of information from misleading content is crucial. The ability to identify trustworthy news outlets and become selective consumers of news is an essential skill for maintaining a healthy democracy. This journey begins with understanding the characteristics that define established news organizations.

Established news outlets typically have a long history of accountability and ethical reporting. They adhere to stringent editorial standards, which include fact-checking processes, transparency in sourcing, and corrections of errors when they occur. For example, newspapers like The New York Times, BBC, and The Guardian, despite occasional criticisms, are often lauded for their commitment to these principles. Their track records demonstrate a consistent adherence to journalistic ethics, which helps in building trust among readers. Familiarizing oneself with such benchmarks can provide a solid foundation for recognizing credible sources.

A diverse media diet is equally important to challenge one's perspectives and overcome echo chambers. Consuming news from various viewpoints not only broadens one's understanding of complex issues but also fosters tolerance and critical thinking. While it is natural to gravitate towards sources that align with personal beliefs, deliberately seeking out alternative perspectives can highlight biases and assumptions. For instance, balancing reports from conservative-leaning outlets like Fox News with those from liberal-leaning sources such as MSNBC can offer a more rounded view of political events. This practice encourages individuals to critically evaluate the information presented and recognize the influence of different editorial slants.

Community-driven journalism plays a pivotal role in establishing trust through local engagement. Local news outlets, often overlooked in favor of national or international media, offer invaluable insights into regional issues and foster a sense of community responsibility. These outlets tend to be more attuned to the specific needs and concerns of their audiences, creating a platform for civic participation and dialogue. Engaging with local journalists and media can help individuals stay informed about their immediate environment and contribute to collective problem-solving. For example, a community newspaper covering city council meetings or local school board decisions can provide residents with actionable information that directly impacts their daily lives.

To effectively navigate the vast ocean of information available online, utilizing research tools and libraries dedicated to reliable knowledge is indispensable. Digital tools such as Google Scholar, JSTOR, and library databases offer access to academic journals and peer-reviewed articles, which are critical for in-depth understanding. Academic journals, in particular, undergo rigorous review processes before publication, ensuring the credibility and accuracy of the content. Libraries, both physical and digital, serve as repositories of verified information and can guide users toward trustworthy resources.

Guidelines: When evaluating sources, consider using fact-checking websites like Snopes, FactCheck.org, and the International Fact-Checking Network. These platforms specialize in verifying news stories and claims, offering clear verdicts on their authenticity.

Another useful strategy is cross-referencing information across multiple reputable sources. If a significant event is reported by several established media outlets with similar details, it is likely to be accurate. Conversely, if only fringe websites with dubious credibility cover a story, it warrants skepticism. Reverse image searches, using tools such as TinEye or Google Images, can verify the origins of photographs and detect manipulated visuals that are commonly used in misinformation campaigns.

Furthermore, academic institutions often provide free access to databases and repositories for students and researchers. Taking advantage of these resources can enhance one's ability to distinguish between well-researched articles and opinion pieces masquerading as factual reports. Universities frequently host public lectures, workshops, and seminars on media literacy, which can be valuable educational opportunities.

Combatting fake news and propaganda

Promoting Fact-Checking Initiatives

One of the most effective strategies to counteract the spread of misinformation is promoting fact-checking initiatives. Fact-checking helps verify the accuracy of information before it is shared widely, reducing the potential impact of false narratives. Community involvement plays a crucial role here. By encouraging community members to participate in fact-checking activities, we can create a collective effort to ensure that only reliable information circulates within our networks.

Educational campaigns are essential for raising awareness about the importance of fact-checking. Workshops, webinars, and local events can be organized to teach individuals how to distinguish between credible and non-credible sources. These sessions can offer practical tips, such as checking the author's credentials, looking for corroborating evidence from multiple sources, and using established fact-checking websites. The more people understand these principles, the more resistant they become to falling for fake news.

Peer education is another powerful tool. Encouraging those who have learned fact-checking techniques to share their knowledge with others can amplify the reach of this initiative. Simple actions, like explaining the process to family members, friends, or colleagues, can help build a community of informed individuals who actively question and verify information. This peer network can transform the way communities handle information, making them more resilient against misinformation.

Developing Critical Dialog

Engaging in meaningful conversations about misinformation without causing confrontation is a skill that can greatly reduce the spread of false information. Developing critical dialog involves creating an environment where respectful and thoughtful exchanges can occur, even when opinions differ. This approach not only enhances understanding but also encourages individuals to evaluate information more critically.

One of the keys to fostering respectful dialogue is active listening. When discussing potentially contentious topics, it's important to listen to the other person's perspective without immediately dismissing it. This can be achieved by asking open-ended questions that encourage further explanation and understanding. For instance, instead of saying, "That's wrong," one might ask, "Can you tell me more about where you heard that?" This approach opens up a conversation rather than shutting it down.

Practicing empathy is equally important. Understanding that people may hold onto misinformation due to deeply ingrained beliefs or fears can help frame the conversation in a more compassionate light. Acknowledging these emotions and gently guiding the discussion towards factual information can make the exchange more productive. It's beneficial to present evidence clearly and calmly, avoiding an aggressive tone that might lead to defensiveness.

Utilizing Social Media Responsibly

Social media platforms are both a blessing and a curse in the fight against misinformation. While they provide unparalleled access to information, they also allow misinformation to spread rapidly. To counteract this, it is essential to understand how sharing patterns can perpetuate false narratives.

One key strategy is implementing pause moments before sharing content. Before clicking the share button, take a moment to consider the source of the information and its credibility. Ask yourself questions like: Is this information verified by reputable sources? Are there any obvious biases? Pausing allows for reflection and reduces the impulse to share potentially harmful content.

Being mindful of the emotional impact of a post is also crucial. Misinformation often thrives on sensationalism and emotional manipulation. If a post evokes a strong emotional reaction—whether it be anger, fear, or joy—it's worth investigating further before sharing. Emotional posts are more likely to be shared hastily and without verification, contributing to the spread of false information.

Furthermore, setting personal guidelines for social media use can help maintain responsible sharing habits. These guidelines might include regularly fact-checking shared content, following a diverse range of credible news sources, and unfollowing accounts known for spreading misinformation. By establishing and adhering to these practices, individuals can significantly reduce their contribution to the spread of false information.

Advocating for Policy Change

While individual actions are vital, systemic change is also necessary to combat misinformation effectively. Advocating for policy change involves engaging in civic activities that shape policies designed to curtail the spread of false information while promoting transparency among tech companies.

Civic engagement can take many forms, from participating in public discussions to lobbying for legislative changes. One effective way to advocate for policy change is through grassroots movements. These movements can amplify public demand for stricter regulations on misinformation and increased accountability for tech giants. By joining forces with like-minded individuals and organizations, concerned citizens can exert significant pressure on policymakers to take action.

Additionally, supporting legislation that promotes transparency and accountability among tech companies is crucial. This includes advocating for laws that require social media platforms to disclose their algorithms and data practices, ensuring that users understand how their information is being used and how content is being prioritized. Transparency in these areas can help mitigate the spread of misinformation by holding tech companies accountable for the content that appears on their platforms.

Furthermore, pushing for policies that support media literacy education can have a long-lasting impact. Incorporating media literacy into school curriculums ensures that future generations are better equipped to navigate the complex information landscape. Educated citizens are less likely to fall prey to misinformation and are more capable of critically evaluating the information they encounter.

The impact of misinformation on democracy

Widespread misinformation poses a severe threat to democratic institutions by eroding public trust. When individuals are constantly exposed to false information, their confidence in government bodies and electoral processes diminishes. This skepticism reaches beyond just one or two institutions; it can taint the entire democratic framework. For example, if misinformation spreads about the integrity of voting systems, people may start doubting election results, which undermines the core of democracy. Robust trust in these institutions is essential for functional governance and citizen participation. Losing this trust can lead to disengagement and apathy, rendering democratic processes ineffective.

Furthermore, misinformation fuels societal polarization by reinforcing existing biases and creating echo chambers. This phenomenon occurs because people tend to seek out information that aligns with their pre-existing beliefs while ignoring contradictory evidence. Social media algorithms amplify this effect by showing users content similar to what they have previously engaged with, thereby deepening divisions. An illustrative case is the divisive rhetoric during elections, where misinformation can exaggerate partisan divides, making compromise and dialogue more challenging. This increased polarization weakens social cohesion and hinders effective policymaking, as leaders find it difficult to garner widespread support for initiatives.

Misinformation also significantly impacts voter behavior, often leading to unfairly swayed election outcomes. If voters make decisions based on false information, the election results do not accurately reflect the will of an informed electorate. For instance, a candidate might be falsely portrayed as having extreme views or being involved in scandalous activities, influencing voters to either support or oppose them without basis in fact. Such scenarios highlight the importance of access to accurate and reliable information for voters to make informed choices. Without this, the underlying principles of democratic elections are compromised, and the legitimacy of elected officials comes into question.

In addressing these challenges, promoting critical engagement through media literacy and critical thinking skills becomes paramount. Media literacy involves the ability to access, analyze, evaluate, and create media in various forms. Teaching citizens how to discern credible sources from unreliable ones empowers them to navigate the complex information landscape more effectively. For example, understanding how to distinguish between opinion pieces and factual reporting helps individuals form well-grounded opinions. Critical thinking goes hand-in-hand with media literacy, enabling citizens to question the motives behind information, recognize biases, and avoid falling prey to manipulative tactics. Enabling a population with these skills fosters an informed and proactive citizenry, better equipped to participate meaningfully in democratic processes.

The necessity for combating misinformation cannot be overstated, considering its ability to disrupt trust in democratic institutions, deepen societal divides, and distort voter behavior. By prioritizing media literacy and critical thinking education, we can create a resilient society capable of discerning truth from falsehood, thus safeguarding democracy. Encouraging open dialogue and fostering environments where diverse perspectives can be discussed critically are crucial steps in this direction. As misinformation continues to evolve, so too must our strategies to counteract it, ensuring that democracy remains robust and inclusive for all citizens.

Another important aspect to consider is the role of technology companies and social media platforms in the dissemination of information. These entities wield significant influence over what information is seen and shared among the public. While some companies have taken steps to curb the spread of misinformation through fact-checking and flagging dubious content, these measures are not universally applied nor always effective. Therefore, it is essential for policymakers to work alongside these technological giants to develop transparent and accountable frameworks that minimize the propagation of false information. Collaboration between governments, tech companies, and civil society organizations can lead to more comprehensive solutions that address the root causes and effects of misinformation.

Moreover, civic education programs should integrate components on identifying misinformation and understanding its implications. Such education would empower future generations with the tools needed to navigate an increasingly digital world. Schools and universities can play a pivotal role in this educational aspect, providing students with practical exercises and real-world examples of how misinformation can influence opinions and behaviors. For instance, analyzing case studies of misinformation campaigns can offer insights into their construction and impact, making students more vigilant consumers of information.

It is also critical to engage communities in active discussions about the detrimental effects of misinformation. Community-based workshops and seminars can provide accessible platforms for individuals to learn and share strategies for identifying and combating false information. These initiatives help build a collective resistance against misinformation, fostering a culture of vigilance and responsibility. Engaged communities are better positioned to support each other in maintaining informational integrity, which is vital for a healthy democracy.

Additionally, the media itself has a responsibility to uphold high standards of journalism and reporting. Ethical journalism practices—such as thorough fact-checking, transparency in sourcing, and clear differentiation between news and opinions—are essential in maintaining public trust. Media outlets should be held accountable for the information they disseminate, with penalties for knowingly spreading falsehoods. By adhering to ethical standards, journalists contribute positively to the public discourse and provide reliable information that citizens can depend on.

This chapter has provided a comprehensive exploration of the strategies essential for identifying and counteracting misinformation in the digital age. By understanding the differences between misinformation and disinformation, readers can better navigate the vast online information landscape. Recognizing tactics such as sensationalized headlines and emotionally charged language helps maintain a critical stance towards news consumption. Moreover, evaluating sources for credibility and understanding the role of algorithms in shaping our perceptions are crucial skills for informed civic engagement.

Promoting media literacy and critical thinking is vital for sustaining a healthy democracy. Engaging with a diverse range of viewpoints, supporting fact-checking initiatives, and fostering respectful dialogues are practical steps to mitigate the impact of false information. Educational institutions and professional workshops can play pivotal roles in cultivating these skills across generations. By staying informed and vigilant, individuals contribute to a more resilient society capable of discerning truth from misinformation, ensuring that democratic processes remain robust and inclusive.

CHAPTER 9

Using Digital Tools for Advocacy

Using digital tools for advocacy involves employing various technologies and online platforms to amplify the efforts of activists and enhance civic engagement within modern democracies. In today's interconnected world, these digital tools have become essential in mobilizing support, raising awareness, and influencing public opinion. From social media campaigns to digital petitions, advocates can reach wider audiences more effectively than through traditional methods alone. By leveraging the power of the internet, individuals and organizations can create impactful movements that resonate on a global scale.

This chapter delves into how social media serves as a potent instrument for advancing advocacy efforts. It explores the strategic use of memorable hashtags and the role influencers play in lending credibility to campaigns. Additionally, the chapter discusses the advantages of live streaming for real-time engagement and the establishment of supportive online networks. The latter part of the chapter addresses the effectiveness of digital petitions and campaigns, highlighting how these tools democratize advocacy by making it accessible to a broader demographic. Furthermore, the chapter outlines best practices for creating compelling online content that drives action and explains the critical importance of cybersecurity in protecting personal data during advocacy activities.

Social Media as a Tool for Activism

Social media has emerged as a powerful tool for advocacy, enabling activists to amplify their efforts, connect with like-minded individuals, and effectively mobilize community engagement. The use of memorable hashtags is one of the most straightforward yet effective methods for campaigns to create a shared language among supporters. A well-crafted hashtag can encapsulate a movement's message, making it easy for people to find and engage with related content. For instance, hashtags like #BlackLivesMatter and #MeToo have not only brought attention to their respective causes but also empowered millions to participate in global conversations.

Hashtags foster a sense of unity and belonging by providing a common platform for dialogue. When a campaign's hashtag trends, it captures the attention of a broader audience, including those who may not have been previously aware of the issue. This broader reach often translates to increased visibility and support for the cause. Moreover, memorable hashtags simplify the process of tracking and measuring the impact of social media campaigns, helping organizers refine their strategies.

Another significant aspect of leveraging social media for advocacy is the involvement of influencers. Influencers lend credibility to initiatives by drawing followers who trust their opinions and expertise. Partnerships with micro-influencers, who have smaller but highly engaged followings, can be particularly effective. These collaborations help frame advocacy messages in relatable ways, making them more accessible to a wider audience. For example, an environmental organization might partner with eco-conscious influencers to promote sustainable practices, thereby reaching individuals who are already interested in green living.

Guideline: To maximize the impact of influencer partnerships, it is essential to choose individuals whose values align with the cause. Authenticity resonates with audiences, so influencers who genuinely care about the issues they promote are more likely to inspire action. Additionally, clear communication of campaign goals and expectations ensures that the message remains consistent and impactful across different platforms.

Live streaming offers another dynamic avenue for real-time engagement. Through live video, advocates can provide transparency, update followers on ongoing efforts, and directly interact with their audience. This real-time interaction enhances the sense of community and immediacy, encouraging viewers to become actively involved. For instance, during live streams of protests or rallies, organizers can share firsthand accounts, answer questions, and rally additional support from viewers who are unable to attend in person.

Guideline: To make the most of live streaming, preparation is key. Advocates should plan their broadcasts in advance, ensuring they have a clear agenda and engaging content. Technical aspects such as internet connection, camera quality, and audio clarity should be tested beforehand to avoid disruptions. Promoting the live stream in advance helps build anticipation and guarantees a larger audience.

Social media also plays a critical role in facilitating supportive online networks. Dedicated groups or pages serve as hubs for resources, updates, discussions, and long-term engagement. These virtual spaces allow advocates to share information, gather valuable feedback, and collaborate on strategies. They also provide a sense of belonging, which is crucial for sustaining momentum in advocacy efforts. For example, Facebook groups dedicated to specific causes enable members to exchange ideas, coordinate actions, and offer mutual support.

Guideline: Creating and maintaining an active online community requires regular engagement from organizers. Posting updates, responding to comments, and encouraging participation helps keep the community vibrant and engaged. Establishing clear guidelines for behavior and discussion ensures a respectful and productive environment where all members feel valued and heard.

Digital Petitions and Campaigns

Digital tools have revolutionized the way advocates can mobilize support and influence decision-makers, with digital petitions and campaigns becoming particularly effective mechanisms for driving change. These tools allow individuals from diverse backgrounds to engage in civic activities, enhancing democratic values through participatory action.

Established platforms like Change.org provide a robust foundation for initiating and promoting petitions. These platforms offer pre-designed templates that simplify the creation process, making it accessible even to those without technical expertise. The structured approach ensures that petitions are clear and compelling, which is crucial for capturing public interest. Additionally, these platforms offer promotional tools that help increase petition visibility. By sharing petitions through social media channels or integrating them into email campaigns, advocates can reach vast audiences quickly and efficiently.

Tracking petition metrics is another essential component of a successful digital campaign. Metrics such as the number of signatures, geographic distribution of signers, and the rate at which a petition gains support can provide valuable insights. These data points help strategize outreach efforts, enabling advocates to target specific demographics or regions that may have a vested interest in the issue at hand. High signature counts can be particularly persuasive when presented to legislators or other decision-makers, demonstrating the broad public support that exists for a particular cause. Furthermore, metrics can help organizers identify trends and adjust their strategies accordingly, ensuring maximal impact.

Coordinating larger campaigns around petitions significantly amplifies their effectiveness. Petition drives can be integrated into broader advocacy initiatives such as letter-writing campaigns, phone banks, and organized rallies. For example, after gathering a substantial number of signatures, advocates might encourage supporters to participate in a coordinated effort to contact their elected representatives. These combined actions exert additional pressure on decision-makers, creating a multifaceted push for legislative or policy changes. The synchronicity of these efforts not only enhances visibility but also creates a sense of urgency and unified purpose among participants.

Updating supporters on the progress of a petition is crucial for maintaining momentum and building trust. Regular updates keep supporters engaged and informed about the status of the initiative, whether it's the number of signatures collected, meetings with legislators, or any media coverage garnered. This transparency fosters a sense of ownership and commitment among supporters, encouraging them to stay involved and contribute further. Moreover, by sharing the successes and setbacks encountered during the campaign, advocates can demonstrate their dedication and adaptability, which can inspire continued backing and participation.

One significant benefit of digital petitions is their ability to galvanize public support quickly. When an issue resonates with people, the ease of signing and sharing a digital petition can lead to rapid accumulation of signatures. This groundswell of support can compel decision-makers to take notice, especially if the petition garners media attention or goes viral on social media. In some cases, the sheer volume of signatures can serve as a powerful testament to the strength of public opinion, making it difficult for policymakers to ignore.

Moreover, digital campaigns are often complemented by personalized stories from those affected by the issue, adding a human element that can be profoundly moving. These narratives can be shared alongside the petition, through blog posts, videos, or social media updates, creating a more comprehensive and emotionally engaging campaign. Personal stories make abstract issues relatable, fostering empathy and a deeper connection to the cause.

Additionally, the accessibility of digital tools means that marginalized voices, which might otherwise struggle to be heard, can find an audience. Platforms like Change.org democratize advocacy by providing everyone, regardless of their resources or background, with the opportunity to initiate meaningful campaigns. This inclusivity strengthens democratic processes by ensuring a wider array of perspectives and concerns are brought to the forefront.

Another critical aspect of utilizing digital tools for advocacy is the potential for real-time engagement and feedback. Supporters can interact with the campaign through comments, shares, and discussions, providing immediate reactions and suggestions. This interactive element allows advocates to gauge public sentiment and adjust their strategies dynamically. For instance, if supporters express confusion or require more information about a specific aspect of the petition, organizers can promptly address these concerns, thereby clarifying the message and strengthening the campaign.

Furthermore, the scalability of digital campaigns means they can grow organically as more people become aware and join the cause. Unlike traditional petitions, which might be constrained by physical barriers or limited distribution channels, digital petitions can reach a global audience. This expansive reach is particularly advantageous for issues that have widespread relevance or require international support, increasing the likelihood of achieving meaningful change.

Creating Impactful Online Content

Producing engaging online content is a cornerstone of effective advocacy in the digital age. With an overload of information accessible at our fingertips, creating impactful and relatable content is key to catching the audience's attention and driving meaningful action. Here, we explore several strategies to achieve this.

Personal stories and visual storytelling play a vital role in making complex issues relatable. By sharing real-life experiences, advocates can evoke empathy and connect on a personal level with their audience. For instance, a campaign focusing on climate change can use the story of a farmer who has faced unpredictable weather patterns, thereby making the abstract issue tangible. The visual component - including photos, infographics, and short videos - enhances this connection by providing immediate emotional impact. Visual storytelling not only simplifies complicated topics but also boosts the likelihood that the content will be shared across social networks, expanding its reach.

Diverse content forms are another essential aspect of modern advocacy. Different people prefer different types of media, and by diversifying content offerings, advocates can reach a broader audience. Articles can provide in-depth analysis and factual data for those interested in comprehensive reads, while videos offer dynamic and visually stimulating summaries of key points. Podcasts present an opportunity to delve deeper into discussions and interviews, appealing to listeners who consume content on the go. Utilizing various formats ensures that the message appeals to varied preferences, increasing engagement and retention rates. For example, a campaign against plastic pollution might release a series of articles detailing the negative impacts, complemented by a podcast featuring experts, and short, impactful videos showcasing affected wildlife.

Clear and persuasive calls to action (CTAs) within content are crucial for guiding audiences on what steps they should take next. A well-crafted CTA should be specific, urgent, and easy to follow, driving immediate responses from the audience. For instance, instead of a vague appeal such as "Help us fight climate change," a more direct approach would be, "Sign our petition today to ban single-use plastics in your community." This specificity gives the audience a clear sense of direction and urgency, making them more likely to act. CTAs can be integrated into all forms of content, whether it is a clickable link in an article, a verbal prompt in a podcast, or an end screen in a video.

Monitoring performance through analytics allows advocates to refine their strategies and optimize outreach efforts based on data insights. Analytics tools can track various metrics such as views, shares, likes, comments, and time spent on content. These insights reveal which types of content are most effective in engaging the audience and driving action. For instance, if a particular video garners significantly higher engagement than others, it could indicate that video content resonates more with the target audience. Using this data, advocates can adjust their content strategy to focus more on high-performing formats and topics. Moreover, analytics can identify peak times for posting, preferred social platforms, and demographic details of the engaged audience, further enhancing targeted outreach.

By combining these strategies, advocates can create compelling and effective online content that not only raises awareness but also encourages proactive engagement. The integration of personal stories and visual elements makes issues relatable and memorable. Offering content in diverse formats caters to different audience preferences, broadening the campaign's reach. Clear CTAs guide audiences toward immediate actions, ensuring that the momentum generated translates into tangible outcomes. Finally, leveraging analytics to monitor and adapt strategies ensures continuous improvement and maximizes the impact of advocacy efforts.

These practices are particularly relevant in today's interconnected world, where digital platforms serve as powerful tools for mobilizing communities and influencing public opinion. As concerned citizens, activists, educators, and political professionals navigate the evolving landscape, producing engaging online content remains a crucial tactic for driving positive change and protecting democratic values. Whether it's initiating grassroots movements or influencing policy decisions, the ability to craft and disseminate compelling content determines the success and sustainability of advocacy campaigns.

Cybersecurity and Protecting Personal Data

In today's digital age, safeguarding personal information and ensuring online security are paramount for advocates engaging in advocacy. Understanding privacy settings and policies is the first step towards informed decision-making. Advocates must familiarize themselves with the terms and conditions of the platforms they use. These documents often outline how data is collected, stored, and shared. By comprehending these aspects, advocates can make conscious choices about the information they share and the platforms they engage with. Additionally, knowing which data is accessible to third parties helps in assessing potential risks.

Advocates should also prioritize implementing strong passwords. Passwords serve as the primary line of defense against unauthorized access. Using complex passwords that include a combination of letters, numbers, and special characters can significantly reduce vulnerability. It's advisable to avoid using easily guessable information, such as birthdays or common words. To further enhance security, advocates should opt for two-factor authentication (2FA). This adds an extra layer of protection by requiring a second form of verification, such as a code sent to a mobile device, in addition to the password.

Regular updates are equally crucial. Software developers frequently release updates to address security flaws and improve functionality. Neglecting these updates can leave a system susceptible to known threats and exploits. Keeping software up-to-date ensures that advocates benefit from the latest security enhancements. Utilizing antivirus programs and firewalls also provides an added layer of defense against malware and other malicious activities.

Acknowledging the risks associated with digital advocacy is essential. Doxxing, hacking, and harassment are prevalent threats that can affect advocates. Doxxing involves the public release of private information, potentially leading to physical harm or emotional distress. Advocates should be cautious about the personal information they share online and consider using pseudonyms where possible. Hacking poses the risk of unauthorized access to confidential information. Advocates should stay vigilant against phishing attempts, which often come in the form of deceptive emails or messages aiming to steal credentials. Harassment, both online and offline, can intimidate advocates and deter them from their missions. Building a support network and having a plan in place to report and counteract harassment can mitigate its impact.

Encrypted communications are vital for protecting sensitive information during advocacy activities. Encryption converts data into a coded format that can only be deciphered by authorized parties. Utilizing encrypted messaging apps, such as Signal or WhatsApp, ensures that conversations remain private and secure from eavesdroppers. For email communications, advocates can use encryption tools like PGP (Pretty Good Privacy) to safeguard content. These measures are particularly important during protests or discussions involving strategic planning, where leaks could jeopardize the safety and effectiveness of advocacy efforts.

Moreover, it is important for advocates to understand the mechanisms and benefits of encryption. Encryption works by encoding the message content, rendering it unreadable to anyone but the intended recipient who has the decryption key. This level of security not only protects communications from potential interceptors but also enhances trust among team members and collaborators. Advocates must ensure that all participants in their communication channels are aware of and adhere to encryption protocols. This collective vigilance fortifies the overall security framework of advocacy initiatives.

To streamline these security practices, advocates can utilize password managers. These tools generate and store strong passwords, reducing the burden of remembering multiple complex passwords. Password managers also facilitate the regular updating of passwords, ensuring continuous protection. Encouraging the use of reputable password managers within advocacy groups can significantly enhance collective security.

Advocates should also cultivate a culture of cybersecurity awareness. Regular training sessions on identifying phishing scams, recognizing suspicious behavior, and responding to online threats can empower advocates to act swiftly and effectively. Establishing clear protocols for reporting and addressing security incidents reduces reaction time and mitigates potential damage.

Navigating the digital landscape requires advocates to be proactive and vigilant. Awareness of privacy settings and policies provides the foundation for making informed choices about data sharing. Implementing robust security measures, such as strong passwords, two-factor authentication, and regular updates, fortifies personal online safety. Recognizing the risks associated with digital advocacy, including doxxing, hacking, and harassment, equips advocates to counteract and mitigate these threats effectively. Embracing encrypted communications safeguards sensitive information, shielding organizers from surveillance and enhancing the overall security of advocacy efforts.

Building Online Communities

Online communities play a crucial role in fostering long-term engagement and support for advocacy efforts. In the digital age, these communities have become indispensable tools for advocates seeking to create lasting change. By understanding their functions and benefits, we can harness their potential to enhance collective knowledge, resilience, and sustained activism.

Dedicated groups or pages on various digital platforms serve as vital resource hubs and discussion forums. These online spaces provide members with access to a wealth of information, including research articles, news updates, and educational materials related to their cause. For instance, environmental advocacy groups frequently use dedicated pages to share scientific studies about climate change, legislation updates, and renewable energy solutions. This concentrated repository of knowledge not only informs members but also enhances their ability to engage effectively with broader audiences and policymakers.

In addition to serving as resource centers, these online communities facilitate dynamic discussions that contribute to collective intelligence. Members can ask questions, exchange ideas, and debate strategies in real-time, fostering a collaborative environment where diverse perspectives are valued. This interaction is fundamental to building a resilient advocacy network. For example, during a campaign to protect public lands, members might discuss different approaches to lobbying local governments, share successful tactics from previous campaigns, and brainstorm innovative protest methods. Such exchanges help advocates remain adaptable and well-informed, enabling them to respond swiftly to new challenges and opportunities.

Another critical aspect of online communities is the mutual support they offer to their members. Advocacy work can be emotionally and mentally taxing, especially when faced with opposition or slow progress. By sharing personal experiences and success stories, members of online communities can uplift one another and maintain morale. For example, a group advocating for mental health reforms might feature testimonials from individuals who have benefited from policy changes, providing tangible proof that their efforts are making a difference. This shared sense of purpose and validation can motivate advocates to persevere, even in the face of setbacks.

Active participation in online communities also ensures sustained engagement beyond immediate campaigns. Unlike traditional advocacy methods, which often dissipate after an initial burst of activity, digital platforms enable continuous interaction and mobilization. Members can stay informed about ongoing issues, participate in regular discussions, and receive updates on new initiatives. For instance, after a successful petition drive, an advocacy group might use their online community to organize follow-up actions, such as letter-writing campaigns or virtual town hall meetings. By keeping the conversation alive, these communities help maintain momentum and prevent the cause from fading into obscurity.

The creation of online hubs promotes a profound sense of belonging and mutual support among activists. Being part of a dedicated group reinforces an individual's commitment to the cause and provides a safe space to share ideas without fear of judgment. This sense of community strengthens the overall advocacy network, as members feel more connected and invested in their collective mission. For example, a human rights advocacy group might create a private forum where members can discuss sensitive topics freely, knowing they are among like-minded individuals. This environment encourages deeper engagement and fosters long-lasting partnerships that extend beyond the digital realm.

Furthermore, the democratizing nature of online communities allows for greater inclusivity and diversity within advocacy efforts. Digital platforms break down geographical barriers, enabling people from different regions and backgrounds to collaborate on common goals. This inclusivity enriches the advocacy movement by incorporating a wide range of experiences and viewpoints.

For instance, a global women's rights organization might connect activists from different continents, allowing them to share cultural insights and develop strategies that are effective across various contexts. This global perspective not only broadens the reach of the movement but also enhances its credibility and influence.

In practice, the impact of online communities can be seen in several notable advocacy successes. The #MeToo movement, for instance, harnessed the power of social media to create a global dialogue about sexual harassment and assault. Online communities provided a platform for survivors to share their stories, garner support, and advocate for systemic change. The movement's widespread reach and sustained momentum were largely due to the active participation of individuals in these digital spaces.

Similarly, environmental advocacy groups have leveraged online communities to coordinate large-scale actions, such as global climate strikes. Young activists like Greta Thunberg have used social media to mobilize millions of supporters worldwide, demonstrating the potential of digital platforms to facilitate grassroots movements. These examples underscore the efficacy of online communities in driving long-term engagement and achieving tangible results.

As we look towards the future, the role of online communities in advocacy is likely to expand further. Advances in technology will continue to provide new tools and platforms for activists to connect, communicate, and collaborate. Virtual reality, for example, could offer immersive experiences that bring advocacy issues to life, engaging audiences in novel ways. Similarly, artificial intelligence might enhance the ability of online communities to analyze data, identify trends, and develop evidence-based strategies.

To maximize the potential of online communities, advocates must remain proactive in cultivating these digital spaces. This involves creating inclusive environments that encourage participation, prioritizing transparency and trust, and continuously adapting to new technological advancements. By doing so, advocacy groups can build robust networks that are capable of sustaining long-term engagement and driving meaningful change.

This chapter has explored the critical role that technology and digital platforms play in enhancing advocacy efforts and civic engagement in modern democracy. By leveraging tools such as hashtags, influencers, live streaming, and online communities, advocates can amplify their messages, reach wider audiences, and foster sustained participation. These methods not only increase visibility but also create spaces for meaningful dialogue and collaboration, strengthening the overall impact of advocacy initiatives.

Additionally, the use of digital petitions and campaigns has proven effective in mobilizing support and influencing decision-makers. The integration of personal stories and multimedia elements adds a compelling human element, making issues more relatable and urgent. Ensuring cybersecurity and protecting personal data remain paramount to maintaining trust and safety within these digital engagements. Overall, this chapter emphasizes the transformative potential of digital tools in driving democratic participation and shaping policy reforms.

CHAPTER 10

Securing America's Future

Securing America's future involves implementing strategies to protect democracy and preserve democratic institutions. A functioning democracy relies on an engaged and informed citizenry actively participating in civic life. Without such involvement, democratic systems can become fragile, opening the door to authoritarianism and the erosion of civil liberties. Hence, strengthening civic engagement is seen as a foundational effort in ensuring the resilience and longevity of democratic institutions.

This chapter will delve into various long-term strategies aimed at safeguarding democracy. We will explore how fostering a culture of civic engagement serves as a bulwark against democratic decay. The discussion will cover community-supported initiatives like town hall meetings and volunteer-driven projects that encourage public participation. Engaging younger generations through comprehensive civic education programs will also be examined, highlighting how early education can instill lifelong habits of participation. Additionally, the role of technology in promoting political engagement and transparency will be discussed, emphasizing digital platforms' potential in broadening civic dialogue. Finally, the chapter will address the importance of building trust in democratic institutions through transparency and accountability measures, underscoring their essential role in maintaining public confidence.

Fostering a Culture of Civic Engagement

Cultivating an active and informed citizenry is fundamental to securing America's democratic future. A resilient democracy thrives on the engagement of its citizens, who must be aware and involved in public affairs. Without this foundation, democratic institutions can falter, leaving society vulnerable to authoritarian tendencies and erosion of rights.

Community-supported initiatives play a pivotal role in fostering public participation. Local programs designed to raise awareness about civic duties and opportunities for involvement are essential. For example, town hall meetings, community forums, and volunteer-driven projects can create spaces where citizens discuss local issues, propose solutions, and work collaboratively to address communal challenges. These initiatives not only enhance individual awareness but also build a sense of collective responsibility. Engaging in these activities helps bridge the gap between citizens and their representatives, fostering a more inclusive and participatory political culture.

Guideline: Communities can establish regular forums and workshops to educate citizens on pressing local issues and encourage them to participate actively in governance processes. This could include organizing monthly town hall meetings, launching local newsletters, or creating online discussion groups dedicated to community concerns.

Engaging younger generations is another critical strategy for cultivating an informed citizenry. Introducing civic education early in schools can have lasting impacts, preparing future voters and instilling lifelong habits of participation. By integrating subjects such as the Constitution, the electoral process, and the importance of voting, educators can inspire students to become engaged citizens. Additionally, encouraging student-led initiatives such as mock elections, debate clubs, and community service projects can provide practical experiences that underscore the value and impact of civic participation.

Guideline: Schools should incorporate comprehensive civic education programs into their curricula, offering courses on government functions, citizen responsibilities, and the significance of voting. Teachers can use interactive methods like simulations of congressional hearings or local government meetings to make learning engaging and impactful.

In today's digital age, technology offers vast opportunities to engage citizens and promote political participation. Leveraging digital platforms can facilitate community dialogue, especially among digital natives who are more accustomed to interacting online. Social media, for instance, can be a powerful tool for mobilizing communities, raising awareness about critical issues, and organizing events. Online petitions, virtual town halls, and interactive webinars can also serve as accessible avenues for political engagement, making it easier for people to express their opinions and contribute to public discourse.

Guideline: Civic organizations should utilize social media and other digital tools to reach broader audiences. Creating informative content, hosting virtual Q&A sessions with local officials, and using data analytics to tailor engagement strategies can significantly enhance participation rates.

Building trust in democratic institutions is paramount for ensuring their effectiveness and legitimacy. Transparency and accountability in governance help strengthen public trust. When citizens believe that their leaders are acting in their best interest and that there are systems in place to hold officials accountable, they are more likely to engage in the democratic process. Transparent decision-making processes, open access to government data, and regular public reporting on governmental activities can demystify operations and reduce skepticism.

Guideline: Governments at all levels can implement policies to enhance transparency and accountability. This may include mandatory disclosures of public officials' financial interests, independent audits of government spending, and public access to legislative proceedings. Establishing ombudsman offices or citizen oversight committees can further ensure that grievances are addressed promptly and fairly.

Promoting an active and informed citizenry is not just the responsibility of public institutions but requires a concerted effort across various sectors of society. Civil society organizations, educational institutions, and the media all play crucial roles in this endeavor. Together, they can create an ecosystem where citizens are continually informed, encouraged, and empowered to participate in democratic processes.

Educational Initiatives and Awareness Programs

Education and awareness are essential tools for sustaining democracy over the long term. By equipping citizens with knowledge, skills, and an informed mindset, we can create a robust foundation that supports democratic values and institutions.

Civic education programs are the cornerstone of this effort. These programs aim to instill civic knowledge and responsibilities in students at various educational levels, ensuring that the principles of democracy are understood from a young age. Incorporating civic education into curricula can take several forms. For instance, primary schools might introduce basic concepts of government and citizenship, encouraging students to understand their role within a democratic society. As students progress to secondary and higher education, these programs can delve deeper into subjects such as constitutional law, civil rights, and the electoral process. By fostering a comprehensive understanding of how democracy functions and what it requires to thrive, civic education programs prepare future generations to be active, responsible participants in their communities and the broader political landscape.

Public awareness campaigns play a crucial role in complementing formal education by reaching a wider audience. These campaigns serve to remind and inform citizens about the importance of civic engagement and staying informed on political matters. One effective strategy is to use multimedia approaches that combine traditional media like television and radio with digital platforms such as social media and websites. These campaigns can spotlight key issues, highlight the importance of voting, and provide information on how to participate in elections and other civic activities. Through compelling narratives and accessible information, public awareness campaigns can significantly boost voter turnout and encourage a more engaged citizenry.

Workshops and training sessions offer another avenue for empowering citizens with practical skills and knowledge. These initiatives can be tailored to different groups, including students, community leaders, and the general public. Workshops focused on advocacy techniques can teach attendees how to organize, communicate effectively, and influence policy decisions. Training on civic duties can cover aspects such as monitoring elections, participating in local government meetings, and understanding legislative processes. By providing hands-on experience and practical tools, these workshops foster a sense of empowerment and responsibility among participants, enabling them to actively contribute to the democratic process.

In today's digital age, utilizing online resources is indispensable for making civic education accessible to a broad audience. Digital platforms provide the flexibility to reach people regardless of geographical constraints, making it easier for citizens to access information at their convenience. Webinars, online courses, and virtual seminars can cover a wide range of topics related to democracy and civic engagement. These resources can be especially beneficial for those who may not have easy access to traditional educational settings. Furthermore, online forums and discussion groups can facilitate the exchange of ideas and experiences, promoting a collaborative learning environment. The integration of interactive elements, such as quizzes and simulations, can enhance engagement and retention of information, making the learning process both informative and enjoyable.

Implementing these strategies requires a collective effort from various stakeholders, including educators, policymakers, non-profit organizations, and the media. Collaboration among these groups ensures that civic education and awareness efforts are comprehensive, inclusive, and effective. Educators play a critical role in shaping curricula and delivering content in engaging ways, while policymakers can support these initiatives through legislation and funding. Non-profit organizations can provide additional resources and support, creating community-based programs that extend beyond the classroom. The media, on the other hand, holds the power to amplify messages and reach diverse audiences, making it a vital partner in public awareness campaigns.

To ensure the success and sustainability of these efforts, continuous evaluation and adaptation are necessary. Assessing the effectiveness of civic education programs, public awareness campaigns, workshops, and online resources allows for ongoing improvements and adjustments to meet changing needs and challenges. Feedback from participants and other stakeholders can provide valuable insights into what works well and what areas require further development. This iterative process helps maintain the relevance and impact of education and awareness initiatives, fostering a resilient and informed democratic society.

Proposing and Supporting Democratic Reforms

Advocating for democratic reforms is crucial to ensure that America's future remains secure, its institutions robust, and its representation inclusive. The necessity of such advocacy cannot be overstated in light of ongoing challenges and potential threats to democracy. By focusing on comprehensive reform strategies, building effective coalitions, engaging in legislative advocacy, and implementing rigorous monitoring and evaluation mechanisms, we can fortify our democratic structures and processes.

To begin with, comprehensive reform strategies are essential in addressing the systemic issues that undermine democratic integrity. These strategies should focus not only on enhancing voter access but also on increasing government transparency. For instance, implementing measures such as automatic voter registration and extended early voting can remove barriers to participation, ensuring that more citizens can exercise their right to vote. Additionally, campaigns to educate voters about their rights and the importance of their participation can further enhance voter turnout.

In terms of government transparency, open data initiatives where government actions and expenditures are made readily available to the public can play a pivotal role. Such transparency mechanisms build trust between the government and its citizens while holding elected officials accountable. This includes easy access to information about legislative sessions, budget allocations, and decision-making processes, which allows the public to stay informed and engaged. Developing proposals that address these core issues can set the foundation for a more resilient and representative democracy.

Building coalitions for reform is another critical aspect of this advocacy effort. By forming alliances among diverse civic groups, reform advocates can amplify their efforts and create a broader base of support. These coalitions can include local community organizations, non-profits, civil rights groups, labor unions, youth associations, and even private sector entities that have a vested interest in maintaining a stable and democratic society. Working together, these groups can launch coordinated campaigns that push for necessary policy changes at both state and federal levels.

One of the key benefits of such coalition-building is the pooling of resources and expertise. Each participating organization brings its unique strengths and perspectives, which can lead to more innovative solutions and greater collective impact. For example, civil rights groups might focus on addressing voter suppression tactics, while environmental groups might advocate for policies that promote governmental accountability in environmental protection. Together, they can create a powerful advocacy network that champions comprehensive democratic reforms.

Legislative advocacy is another vital component in this process of securing America's democratic future. Grassroots lobbying efforts, where ordinary citizens engage directly with lawmakers, play an instrumental role in influencing policy outcomes. Citizens can organize town hall meetings, participate in public hearings, and use social media platforms to communicate directly with their elected representatives about their concerns and priorities. This direct engagement ensures that legislators are aware of the public's demand for reform and are held accountable for their actions.

Developing a clear and compelling narrative around the need for democratic reforms can help galvanize public support and drive legislative change. This involves articulating the specific problems with current systems, proposing practical and evidence-based solutions, and highlighting the benefits of proposed reforms. Effective legislative advocacy requires persistence and the strategic use of various communication channels to reach both policymakers and the general public, ensuring that the call for reform is loud and sustained.

Finally, monitoring and evaluation are indispensable in ensuring the effectiveness and accountability of reform measures. Establishing independent bodies tasked with assessing the implementation and outcomes of reforms is crucial. These bodies should be empowered to conduct thorough and transparent evaluations, publishing regular reports on their findings. Such evaluations help identify areas of improvement and hold government officials accountable for achieving reform objectives.

For example, an independent commission could be created to oversee election practices and ensure compliance with new voter access laws. This commission would review electoral processes, investigate complaints, and provide recommendations to improve fairness and accessibility. Similarly, transparency initiatives could be evaluated by watchdog organizations that monitor government disclosures and track progress towards greater openness.

The importance of these monitoring efforts cannot be understated. Independent evaluations not only measure the success of reforms but also build public trust in the democratic process. When citizens see that reforms are being implemented effectively and that there is accountability for any lapses, their confidence in democratic institutions is strengthened.

Maintaining Vigilance and Ongoing Advocacy Efforts

Establishing Watchdog Organizations

The first step in safeguarding democracy is the establishment of watchdog organizations. These groups play a crucial role in monitoring political activities and ensuring government transparency. Watchdog organizations serve as the eyes and ears of the public, holding elected officials accountable for their actions.

A prime example of an effective watchdog organization is Transparency International, which works globally to combat corruption and promote integrity within government institutions. By meticulously documenting instances of malpractice and disseminating this information to the public, such organizations help maintain a level of scrutiny imperative for a healthy democracy. In the United States, the Center for Public Integrity performs similar functions by investigating and reporting on various governmental operations and policies.

To form a successful watchdog organization, it is essential to assemble a dedicated team possessing expertise in law, journalism, data analysis, and public policy. Clear objectives must be established, focusing on specific areas such as campaign finance, lobbying activities, or legislative processes. Funding can be secured through donations, grants, and membership fees, ensuring that the organization remains independent and unbiased.

Public engagement is also vital. Regular reports and findings should be made accessible through various media channels, social networks, and public forums. This transparency not only informs citizens but also empowers them to take action when necessary. Ultimately, watchdog organizations strengthen democratic institutions by fostering accountability and deterring corruption.

Engaging in Regular Dialogue with Leaders

Another critical aspect of defending democracy involves engaging in regular dialogue with leaders. Open communication channels between citizens and their representatives are fundamental to a functioning democracy. This engagement ensures that the voices of the people are heard and considered in the decision-making process.

Organizing town hall meetings and public forums provides opportunities for direct interaction between constituents and elected officials. Such events allow citizens to ask questions, express concerns, and provide feedback on policies and initiatives. For instance, the British tradition of "MP surgeries" offers a model for regular and structured interaction where Members of Parliament meet with constituents to discuss issues affecting their local communities.

Beyond physical meetings, leveraging technology can enhance dialogue. Platforms like social media, online petitions, and virtual town halls expand the reach and accessibility of these conversations. Engaging younger demographics who are more comfortable with digital communication tools ensures broader participation across different age groups.

Effective dialogue requires preparation and strategy. Citizens should come equipped with knowledge of current issues and proposed policies. Organizers can facilitate productive discussions by setting clear agendas and guidelines, ensuring respectful and constructive exchanges. Elected leaders, in turn, must commit to being receptive and responsive to citizen input.

Campaigning for Continued Rights Protection

Continuous advocacy for the protection of constitutional rights and civil liberties is another pillar of democratic integrity. Rights protection campaigns are essential, particularly during periods of political change, when there may be attempts to undermine existing freedoms.

Organizations like the American Civil Liberties Union (ACLU) exemplify how sustained efforts can safeguard individual rights. The ACLU has played a crucial role in various landmark cases, challenging laws and policies that infringe upon civil liberties, from freedom of speech to privacy rights.

Grassroots movements are instrumental in campaigning for rights protection. Mobilizing citizens through rallies, petitions, and awareness campaigns creates pressure on policymakers to uphold democratic principles. For example, the Black Lives Matter movement has successfully brought attention to issues of racial inequality and police brutality, prompting legislative changes and increased public awareness.

Education and outreach programs further bolster advocacy efforts. Informing citizens about their rights and the importance of protecting them fosters a society ready to stand against any erosions of freedom. Collaborations with schools, community centers, and media outlets can disseminate information widely, ensuring that diverse populations are informed and engaged.

Building a Culture of Accountability

Finally, promoting a culture of accountability is indispensable for preserving democratic values. A society committed to challenging undemocratic practices and upholding norms is less likely to tolerate misconduct from its leaders.

A culture of accountability begins with individual responsibility. Citizens must recognize their role in maintaining democratic standards, whether through voting, civic participation, or staying informed on policy issues. Educational campaigns that emphasize the significance of each person's contribution to democracy can instill this sense of duty.

Institutional mechanisms are also critical. Independent bodies tasked with auditing government actions, such as ombudsman offices and ethics commissions, provide checks and balances within the system. These institutions investigate complaints, enforce regulations, and recommend corrective actions, ensuring that no one is above the law.

Media plays a crucial role in fostering accountability. Investigative journalism uncovers abuses of power and brings them to public attention. Strong legal protections for journalists and whistleblowers are necessary to support their work and ensure they can operate without fear of retribution.

Furthermore, creating spaces for public discourse, where ideas can be freely exchanged and debated, reinforces accountability. Universities, think tanks, and civic organizations can host debates, lectures, and discussions that encourage critical thinking and evaluate policy impacts.

Leveraging Technology for Democracy

Technology holds significant potential in bolstering democratic principles and processes. One of the most promising aspects in this regard is utilizing digital platforms for civic dialogue. Online forums and social media have revolutionized how citizens engage in discussions about civic rights and responsibilities. These platforms enable the creation of virtual spaces where people from diverse backgrounds can exchange ideas, debate policies, and foster mutual understanding. By lowering the barriers to participation, digital platforms ensure that more voices are heard, creating a richer and more inclusive discourse. Furthermore, these platforms can host live-streamed debates, town hall meetings, and Q&A sessions with public officials, bringing political conversations directly to citizens' screens.

However, fostering constructive civic dialogue online requires careful moderation and the development of healthy community guidelines. Ensuring respectful and fact-based discussions can prevent misinformation and inflammatory rhetoric from derailing productive conversations. Many organizations have started employing dedicated moderators and advanced algorithms to flag inappropriate content promptly, thereby maintaining a focus on meaningful dialogue.

Another critical avenue through which technology supports democracy is the implementation of civic tech tools. These tools play a pivotal role in encouraging political participation and streamlining voting processes. Mobile apps and websites can provide voters with indispensable information, such as registration deadlines, polling locations, and candidate profiles. For instance, applications like TurboVote and Rock the Vote help citizens register to vote and stay informed about upcoming elections.

Additionally, technologies like blockchain are being explored for secure and transparent voting systems. Blockchain's tamper-proof nature ensures that each vote cast is recorded permanently and cannot be altered, addressing concerns about electoral fraud. Pilot projects in countries like

Estonia have shown the potential benefits of such systems, highlighting increased voter turnout and trust in the electoral process.

Online educational content is another vital component in supporting democratic principles. Creating and curating reliable digital resources can make civic knowledge widely accessible to everyone. Websites, apps, and online courses offer interactive ways to learn about government functions, electoral processes, and individual rights and responsibilities. Platforms like Khan Academy and Coursera provide free or low-cost courses on civics, allowing learners to gain a deeper understanding of democracy at their own pace.

Furthermore, initiatives like iCivics, founded by former Supreme Court Justice Sandra Day O'Connor, offer engaging games and activities that teach students about government and citizenship. These resources not only educate but also inspire active participation in democracy by making learning fun and relevant. As a result, individuals can become more informed citizens, capable of critically evaluating political messages and participating meaningfully in public life.

Outreach strategies must evolve to cater to digital natives, ensuring broad engagement across all demographics. The younger generation, having grown up with technology, responds differently to traditional outreach methods. Tailoring strategies to meet them where they are—primarily online—can significantly enhance engagement. Social media campaigns, influencer partnerships, and interactive multimedia content can capture the attention of younger audiences and motivate them to participate in civic activities.

Moreover, personalized communication through data analytics can make outreach efforts more effective. By understanding the preferences and behaviors of different demographic groups, organizations can craft targeted messages that resonate with specific audiences. For instance, using Instagram stories to share behind-the-scenes looks at political campaigns or TikTok videos to explain policy positions in brief, engaging formats can draw in younger voters and encourage them to take action.

Real-world examples illustrate the impact of these digital strategies. During the 2020 U.S. presidential election, campaigns extensively used social media platforms to reach potential voters. Both major parties leveraged Twitter, Facebook, and Instagram to share messages, mobilize supporters, and counter misinformation. These efforts were complemented by grassroots movements like Black Lives Matter, which used digital tools to organize protests, spread awareness, and drive voter registration efforts.

Summarizing the chapter, it's clear that long-term strategies for defending democracy involve fostering a culture of active civic engagement and education. By encouraging informed participation through community-supported initiatives, regular forums, and digital tools, we can bridge the gap between citizens and their representatives. Educating younger generations and employing technology to facilitate political involvement are crucial steps in ensuring that democratic processes remain robust and inclusive. Transparent governance and accountability also build public trust, making it essential for institutions to maintain open communication with the citizenry.

Furthermore, advocating for democratic reforms, forming coalitions, and engaging in legislative advocacy play significant roles in fortifying our democratic structures. Monitoring and evaluating these efforts through independent bodies ensure that reforms are effective and trustworthy. By promoting a culture of accountability and leveraging technology for civic dialogue, we can create a resilient society poised to protect democratic values. The collaboration among educators, civil organizations, and policymakers is vital to sustaining these initiatives, ensuring that democracy thrives for future generations.

CONCLUSION

As we come to the end of this exploration, it is crucial to reflect on the vital themes and insights we have delved into throughout this book. We have thoroughly examined Project 2025, providing a detailed analysis that exposes its complexities and potential implications for our democratic institutions. We've also confronted various threats against our fundamental rights, emphasizing the peril they pose to the bedrock of democracy. It is evident that an informed citizenry stands as the pillar upon which a thriving democracy is built. The knowledge and understanding gained from these discussions are not just academic; they hold real-world significance and urgency.

Our journey through these pages has underscored the importance of each theme in relation to the overarching goal of protecting democracy. The intricacies of political strategies, the fragility of our rights, and the power dynamics at play all lead to one undeniable truth: awareness and education are the first steps toward safeguarding democratic values. By grasping the nuances of these issues, we equip ourselves with the tools necessary to defend against encroachments on our liberties.

But knowledge alone is insufficient without action. It's time to translate understanding into proactive measures. Change begins at the individual level. Each reader holds the potential to spark meaningful transformation within their community. Whether it's engaging in dialogue about political issues, attending local town hall meetings, or participating in grassroots campaigns, every small effort contributes to a larger wave of civic engagement. These actions, though seemingly modest, collectively have the power to fortify our democratic structures.

Consider the impact of a single vote, the ripple effect of an informed conversation, or the influence of a well-organized community event. Each of these acts represents a commitment to preserving democratic ideals. History has shown us that significant societal shifts often begin with the concerted efforts of individuals united by a common purpose. Your role in this ongoing narrative is indispensable. Remember, democracy isn't a spectator sport; it requires our active participation.

Sustained involvement in community affairs extends beyond mere election cycles. This book advocates for an enduring commitment to civic engagement. Democracy resembles a garden; it demands regular nurturing and vigilance. Just as gardeners tend to their plants to ensure they thrive, citizens must remain continuously engaged in local, state, and national issues. This persistent attention guarantees that the seeds of democracy are not just planted but are cultivated and flourish over time.

Community forums, public debates, advocacy groups, and volunteer opportunities are just a few avenues through which sustained engagement can be realized. By immersing ourselves in these activities, we contribute to a dynamic and responsive democratic society. It's about more than casting a ballot every few years; it's about being an active participant in the daily discourse that shapes our nation's future. Engaged citizens are the lifeblood of democracy, breathing vitality into its principles and practices.

Looking forward, envision what a robust, participatory democracy could resemble if each individual applies the knowledge and insights garnered from this book. Imagine a society where every voice is valued, where diverse communities actively participate in shaping governance, and where democratic values serve as a unifying force. Such a future is achievable, but it hinges on our collective commitment to continuous learning and active involvement.

This vision includes schools that foster critical thinking and civic responsibility, communities that encourage open dialogue and mutual respect, and leaders who prioritize transparency and accountability. It pictures a democracy that evolves with its people, adapting to new challenges while maintaining its core principles of equality, justice, and freedom.

Yet, achieving this vision requires perseverance in the face of adversity. The road ahead may be fraught with obstacles, but it is navigable with determination and solidarity. Challenges will undoubtedly arise, but they should be met with resilience and a steadfast belief in the power of collective action. In moments of doubt, recall the lessons drawn from this book and the historical examples of democratic resilience and triumph.

In essence, this conclusion serves as a call to action and a beacon of hope. Armed with the insights and knowledge provided, you stand ready to contribute meaningfully to the preservation and enhancement of democratic values. Each effort, no matter how small, plays a crucial role in the larger tapestry of civic life. Together, we can forge a future where democracy thrives, not merely as a form of government, but as a shared way of life that underscores our commitment to common good and mutual respect.

Let us go forth with renewed vigor and dedication, understanding that the fate of democracy resides not in distant halls of power but in the hands of everyday citizens like you and me. Our collective effort will shape the contours of our political landscape, ensuring that democratic ideals remain vibrant and resilient for generations to come.

FREE SUPPLEMENTARY RESOURCES

Are you looking to actively participate in and rejuvenate American democracy?

Our book, *Project 2025 - A Citizen's Guide to Saving American Democracy*, is your essential guide, offering insightful strategies and actionable steps that every citizen can take. Whether you're deeply involved in politics or just starting to understand your role in democracy, this book is crafted to empower you to make meaningful change.

But there's more! To deepen your understanding and engagement, we're providing an exclusive bonus resource available for download—completely free. Don't miss this opportunity to redefine your civic duties and discover impactful ways to contribute to our democracy!

Use QR code to claim your bonus:

Best regards,

Emily Carter Lee

www.ingramcontent.com/pod-product-compliance
Lightning Source LLC
Chambersburg PA
CBHW062218220526
45471CB00009B/3257